Research Foundations

In memory of Greg Kalkanoff, a great friend who knew that we're all pretty bizarre even if some of us are just better at hiding it.

Research Foundations

How Do We Know What We Know?

Douglas Woodwell

University of Indianapolis

Los Angeles | London | New Delhi
Singapore | Washington DC

Los Angeles | London | New Delhi
Singapore | Washington DC

FOR INFORMATION:

SAGE Publications, Inc.

2455 Teller Road

Thousand Oaks, California 91320

E-mail: order@sagepub.com

SAGE Publications Ltd.

1 Oliver's Yard

55 City Road

London EC1Y 1SP

United Kingdom

SAGE Publications India Pvt. Ltd.

B 1/I 1 Mohan Cooperative Industrial Area

Mathura Road, New Delhi 110 044

India

SAGE Publications Asia-Pacific Pte. Ltd.

3 Church Street

#10-04 Samsung Hub

Singapore 049483

Copyright © 2014 by SAGE Publications, Inc.

Printed in the United States of America

Library of Congress Cataloging-in-Publication Data

Woodwell, Douglas.

Research foundations : how do we know what we know? / Douglas Woodwell.

pages cm

Includes bibliographical references and index.

ISBN 978-1-4833-0674-2 (pbk. : alk. paper) — ISBN 978-1-4833-3405-9 (epub)

ISBN 978-1-4833-3406-6 (xml) — ISBN 978-1-4833-3407-3 (web pdf) 1.

Social sciences—Research—Methodology. 2. Research—Methodology. 3. Interdisciplinary research—Methodology. I. Title.

H62.W665 2013

001.4—dc23   2013031293

This book is printed on acid-free paper.

Acquisitions Editor: Helen Salmon

Editorial Assistant: Kaitlin Coghill

Production Editor: Brittany Bauhaus

Copy Editor: QuADS Prepress (P) Ltd.

Typesetter: C&M Digitals (P) Ltd.

Proofreader: Ellen Brink

Indexer: Diggs Publication Services, Inc.

Cover Designer: Candice Harman

Marketing Manager: Nicole Elliott

MIX
Paper from
responsible sources
FSC® C014174

13 14 15 16 17 10 9 8 7 6 5 4 3 2 1

Brief Contents

Detailed Contents

List of Figures and Tables

Preface

I don't know what they want me to do!

It can be a frustrating and disorienting feeling to be asked to design and/ or execute a research project from scratch. Whether a scholar or student, we have all been there. I'll never forget as a graduate student being told by my advisor that my research needed a "model." After working on my model for the weekend, I brought it back to him, confident that I had put together some really good research only to be told, "It's pretty good, but you still need a model." Ugh.

Of course, that was just one of many frustrations. Other professors told me I needed to develop case studies or conduct ethnographic research. I didn't know what they really meant. As for the statistical approaches that represented the central thrust of my research, well, don't worry "you'll figure it out."

I delved into the libraries at my university, checking out every social science methodology book I could find. Most books involved in-depth discussions of approaches that seemed unrelated to anything I was researching. Other books were intimidating biblical-sized tomes that covered everything and anything but were as overwhelming as they were unapproachable. I eventually got through my dissertation project, but it seemed like the process was a lot more difficult than it needed to be. I never did find a methodology book that worked for me.

This is the book that I wish that I had read back then. In this book, I present a way of mentally framing research in a way that is understandable and approachable while also discussing some of the more specific issues that will aid students in understanding the options available when pursuing research. It is my hope that you as the reader, whether you are an undergraduate or graduate student, a professional or a scholar, or someone simply interested in how research leads to new discoveries, will find that this book helps crystallize your thinking about how we know what we know and how we go about finding out about those things we do not know.

While at certain points I discuss in detail some commonly used research methods, my primary goal in this work is to convey an intuitive and easy-to-understand framework for understanding how research methodologies as a whole fit together and make intuitive sense. Many scholars do not even understand the basic, common sense, nature of how research methodologies guide the search for answers about the world. For some, methodological issues are often thought of as an abstraction or worse, dismissed as a distraction. Furthermore, among many in the social sciences and humanities, in particular, methodological study is simply conflated with quantitative methods that represent a big "turnoff" for the nonmathematically inclined.

Some scholars have put in great efforts defending their own research traditions while pooh-poohing the approaches of others. Much of the "Methodensteite," or "methods conflict" that has reared its head over the years, particularly in the social sciences, has been based on an inadequate understanding of what different research approaches bring to the table and how different types of research questions require different methods of inquiry.

Yet much fruitful research has been conducted by bringing together different methodological traditions and examining research questions in new and interesting ways. For such cross-disciplinary and cross-methodological efforts to be successful, however, scholars need to understand research in a more holistic and more intuitive fashion. The goal of scholars and students should be to achieve a better intuitive and logical understanding of methodological design writ large rather than simply practicing something of an imitative approach to methods particular to their fields. Students and scholars confused by the morass of disjointed terminology and abstract concepts associated with research methodology are likely to benefit from the broader approach to research I take in this book.

My own training is in the social sciences, which in some ways represent a methodological middle ground between the contextual-minded humanities and the universal pursuits of those in the natural sciences. A well-trained social scientist might sometimes be viewed as a jack-of-all-trades and master-of-none, but the exposure to a wide spectrum of research questions and methodologies means that social scientist researchers are well positioned to understand the broad variety of research traditions that exist across fields.

Although many of the examples that I use in this book and some of the methods that I focus on are social science oriented, general methodological approaches are not the exclusive domain of certain types of research. The "big picture" of research I discuss is relevant across the humanities and social and natural sciences. Ultimately, pursuing answers to research questions in the most sensible way is not something that is specific to particular fields of study but rather an exercise in thoughtful problem solving that best addresses the subject at hand, regardless of a researcher's specialization.

Research is a collaborative effort, and this book is no exception. There are many people who gave their helpful suggestions, time, and support. I would like to thank Sage, the good people who work there, and the outside reviewers who worked with them to provide a wealth of suggestions. These reviewers, whose research specialties covered a wide variety of fields, included James R. Anthos of South University, Paul Boyd of Johnson & Wales University, R. David Frantzreb II of the University of North Carolina at Charlotte, Monica B. Glina of Montclair State University, Karen Larwin of Youngstown State University, John Mitrano of Central Connecticut State University, David Vanata of Ashland University, and Maria Victoria Guglietti of Mount Royal University. Any remaining mistakes and shortcomings are, of course, my own.

Two of my colleagues also took on the exhaustive task of reviewing earlier versions of my manuscript. I offer my sincere appreciation to Joe Hansel, of the University of Indianapolis's School of Psychological Sciences, and Milind Thakar, of the Department of History and Political Science, for their efforts.

Despite the best efforts of the above individuals, any errors or misconceptions contained within this book, and there are certain to be a few, should be considered entirely the fault of the author.

I would also like to especially thank Sharon Goetz, who has now taken the time to help cross the t's and dot the i's for two of my book manuscripts. Her time, support, and friendship have been invaluable in recent years.

Many of my students have also offered helpful insights on what works and what does not work in this text. Several of them, including Wesley Cate and Ben Waddell, expended extra effort in helping improve the writing in this book.

I might also never have begun this project had it not been for a conversation with Chinyelu Lee on a balcony in downtown Washington, D.C., five years ago. Thanks Chu, for both the inspiration and the friendship.

Last, but far from least, I would like to thank Sara Bremer Sale, Kim Deckman, Guin Holman, Katy Mann, Lindsay Shoger, and the rest of the crew at the Rehabilitation Hospital of Indiana. Partway through the process of authoring this book, I was permanently paralyzed by a rare abnormality of the blood vessels in my spinal cord. I was fortunate to have such a competent and supportive group help me piece things back together.

Please consider donating to www.christopherreeve.org or similar organizations dedicated to research into repairing spinal cord injuries and making a better life for those living with one.

About the Author

Douglas Woodwell is an associate professor of international relations in the Department of History and Political Science at the University of Indianapolis. He received his BA in international studies at American University, his MA in German and European Studies at Georgetown University, and his PhD in political science at Yale University. His earlier works include articles written for international relations journals and the World Bank as well as the book *Nationalism in International Relations*.

PART I

Overview

Visualizing Research

Overview

This chapter begins by defining the concepts of research and methodology. It presents a model of research processes that links different types of research activities into a unified whole. It briefly discusses each of the steps involved in research, starting with the importance of devising a good research question at the outset of a research project.

Introduction

How do we know what we know? If you live in a developed country, you probably live within a knowledge-based economy within an interconnected knowledge-based world. You depend on knowledge-based products in your daily life: things like computers, medicines, and the bridges and roads that you use on the way to work. Your government enacts policies intended for the public good based, sometimes at least, on expert knowledge about the economy and environment. Your very self-identity and values are conditioned to some degree by a cultural milieu that is heavily influenced by scholars from fields like history, political science, and education.

The discovery of new knowledge is, of course, not just a modern phenomenon. For thousands of years, people have been cooperating to learn new things and to build on the knowledge of their predecessors. Sometimes, the process of discovery has involved massive corporate undertakings, strict protocols, and expensive experiments. Other times, solitary investigators and innovators have blazed new trails of discovery with little more than patience and a curious mind. The one thing that we can be sure about, however, is that mankind will know a little more tomorrow than they know today.

This book is about how people go about understanding how things work. It is through the process of **research**[1] that people pursue knowledge about those things they do not understand, but want to. What sets research apart from other types of learning is that it represents a systematic and intentional effort to answer questions and learn more about a specific subject. We learn things all the time from our environment and through our interactions with others. Experience often confers knowledge without us ever specifically seeking it out.

Research, however, is the process of intentionally seeking out knowledge for the specific purpose of understanding what and why things have happened or are happening. A researcher sets out on a quest to accumulate knowledge and then understands what the knowledge represents. Sometimes, the subject is a narrow one about a particular place, thing, or event, and other times, research involves the effort to understand how things behave in general.

How a researcher best learns about a subject depends on the type of subject they are investigating. Some subjects are best understood by observing them in person, others through rigorous and laborious number crunching and analysis. The subject of **methodology** involves understanding how researchers most sensibly match the way they go about obtaining knowledge with the questions they are trying to answer. With appropriate methodological choices, researchers maximize their approaches to information gathering while minimizing the biases that would accompany less formal attempts to interpret the information that has been gathered.

Research "methodology" refers to a broader idea than the more specific term research "method." Methodologies act as the overarching blueprint for the innumerable types of specific methods that researchers employ in specific disciplines to uncover new information. In military terms, methods are like tactics, and methodologies are like strategies.

While some books may focus on specific methods used in certain fields, I focus more in this work on the "big picture" of how methodologies in different fields interrelate with one another and pursue common goals, albeit in somewhat different ways depending on the questions under

---

1. A glossary appears at the end of this book that provides succinct definitions of the bold terms.

investigation. I discuss general approaches to collecting information and how that information can be used to build different types of causal theories. I also discuss how some researchers go about testing and evaluating theories and what theories can teach us about the world around us.

Few, if any, efforts have been undertaken in the past to address the "big picture" of research across fields. Even scholars who might rightly view themselves as experts in a particular research tradition are often poorly versed in what is happening outside the silo of their field or subfield. Scholarship in general, however, benefits when researchers are well versed in a variety of disciplinary-born approaches and how research questions might be addressed in a variety of ways.

A major goal of this book is to take a step back, start from the beginning, and provide a simple outline of research in general. The process of demystifying research methodology begins by visualizing its constituent parts.

Visualizing Research

Figure 1.1 provides the basic outline for this book, represents a helpful model for understanding the general progress of research as it unfolds, and, most important, displays the manner in which all research is ultimately interconnected. It reflects a holistic, "bird's-eye" view of research as it takes place across different fields and traditions.

One reason that research methodologies seem so "abstract" to many students and scholars has to do with the relation of different methodologies to one another. Picking the best way to address a particular research question is very difficult with a "toolbox approach" that often entails utilizing a particular jargon-laden method and applying it to a problem without much consideration of the "big picture." The research model boils down to the essential features of research, whether **qualitative** or **quantitative**, inductive or deductive, or theoretical or applied. As I describe the different elements of research presented in the model, the reader should refer back to the model frequently to understand how different types of research "fit together" into an integrated picture of knowledge creation.

No single research project employs all of the different steps reflected in the model. Research projects differ in focus and scope depending on the research question they are meant to address. Although some of the more ambitious projects may draw on a variety of methodological steps, it is more common that a project utilizes approaches found in specific areas of the model. To understand how to approach a problem, however,

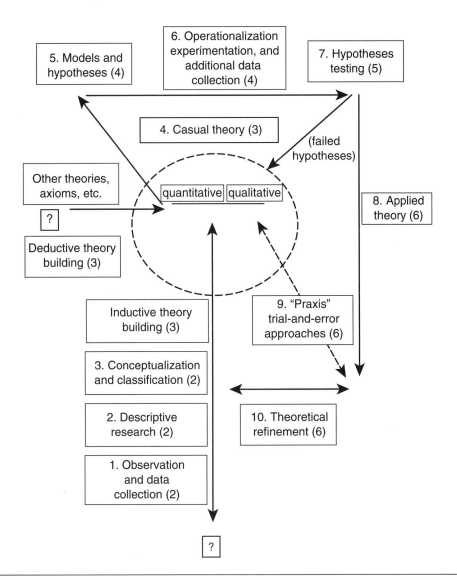

Figure 1.1:   A model of the research process

Chapters covering each topic are noted in (#).

it is necessary for scholars to understand what research options are available to them, which options are most appropriate, the limitations of different approaches, and how different approaches are suited for different types of research questions.

The Research Question

In its earliest stages, research begins with a question or a set of questions about an occurrence that a researcher wishes to understand better. Thus, the first step in coming up with a research question is to find an interesting question. Research proceeds much more effectively when the researcher is motivated by curiosity. Of course, if only the researcher finds the question interesting and no one else does, it might not be the ideal research topic. The best research topics are often those that answer questions that have not been investigated previously or that aim to rectify or verify previous investigations that may have yielded inconclusive or questionable results.

Practical considerations also are important to take into account before conducting research. For instance, is the question something that can be answered given the time and resources available? Plans to undertake a sophisticated statistical analysis are unlikely to proceed very far without the appropriate computer software, just as a medical study is unlikely to go very far without appropriate laboratory equipment. Even something as seemingly "simple" as opinion polling can require immense human resources and time to conduct convincingly.

Another practical consideration involves the scope of the investigation. The process of coming up with a research question often begins, but doesn't end, with an interest in a broad topic. It is impossible to count how many times a student has approached me with a research question saying something like "I'm interested in conflict in Africa." The research into such topics could easily be imagined as filling a multivolume set of books. Broad topics can be winnowed down to more manageable questions by asking specific questions about what time periods, areas, and subject matter interest a researcher.

It is also helpful to think about what the research will accomplish methodologically. Does a researcher want to build his or her own theoretical argument based on original research into a subject? Does the researcher want to test other competing theories that might already exist and determine which seems to hold the most explanatory value? Is the research case specific, or does it examine broad trends in human or natural behavior?

Two problematic types of research questions I have heard from students in the past have involved a desire to (1) "prove" something that fits their preexisting beliefs and (2) "show" why governments, institutions, and people "should" take action in favor of an issue they believe in.

Unfortunately, neither of these "questions" represents a very good start to the research process. The problem with the first type of question is that it is not really a question but, rather, an expression of a desire to confirm a preexisting belief. It is important not to set out seeking a particular desirable conclusion before the process of discovering new information has even begun. Failing to keep an open mind warps research by transforming understanding into rationalization.

Research is also not, in and of itself, simply an exercise in ethical argumentation. No one can research the rightness or wrongness of beliefs divorced from fact. That is not to say that the goals of research need necessarily be value neutral—far from it. However, to argue what should happen, a researcher must first understand what is happening and why it is happening.

Even after an appropriate research question has been settled on, that question is likely to subsequently change, grow, and/or become further refined as the process of uncovering new information progresses. New understandings are often likely to lead a researcher down new avenues of inquiry in a process that is, during the early stages in particular, often organic and circular.

The Process of Research

The research model (Figure 1.1) that I propose for the purpose of visualizing research begins with research questions (labeled "?") and then lays out the sensible progression of research in a largely linear step-by-step fashion. For each point, I discuss the broad outlines of the type of research represented by the step and some of the main terminology associated with the traditions being discussed. The directional arrows tying each point with others represent the logical flow of one step into another.

The research process is, however, not always an exclusively linear "a to b" process. For instance, theories are built on data, while the process of data collection may also be guided by theory. This cyclical dance between theory and data that is characteristic of theory building is represented by the two-way directionality of the arrow tying together the earlier steps of the research model. Other steps, such as the deduction of hypotheses from existing bodies of theory, are represented by one-way arrows that indicate the logical unidirectional progression of the research process in these areas.

The following points highlight the different steps of the research process model as represented and numbered in Figure 1.1. The overview of the model I present below highlights some of the basic elements of research and terminology I use in this book. The rest of the chapters of this book explain each area in much greater detail.

1. All knowledge originates in some form with *observation and data collection*, even if some scholarly research projects utilize information that has already been collected by someone else. The first task of research involves the collection of **data**. While many associate the term *data* with statistical and other quantitative research, the term encompasses any type of information that has been created or gleaned by a researcher from the world. The word data, Latin for "something given," can represent anything from "memory, perception, hearsay" that "are usually (though often wrongly) taken to be true" (Bunge, 1996, p. 85) to spreadsheets full of numerical entries.

Data attempt to represent facts, but the terms are not synonymous. Facts are what exist; they are the true descriptors of the underlying nature of things. Data are information that researchers have translated and filtered from their observations in an attempt to reproduce facts. Unlike facts, data can be correct or incorrect, can be measured more precisely or less, or cannot be really measured at all.

Data are filtered or "made" by a researcher who is drawing from his or her environment through **observation** or experimentation. All data that derive from the effort to reproduce concrete facts are **empirical** data. Empirical data reflect factual information that is measurable, observable either directly or indirectly, and usually tangible. Other nonempirical data can involve attempts to reproduce perceptions or intangible interactions among individuals. Such data form the cornerstone of **interpretivist** and **constructivist approaches**.

In Chapter 2, I cover a range of topics related to observational research. The first part of the chapter is divided into sections that deal with quantitative data collection and less empirical-oriented qualitative data collection. I discuss three major sources of "observable" information: (1) firsthand observation; (2) "mediated" information taken from third-party sources such as TV, radio, and print; and (3) data collected through interviews and surveys.

2. **Descriptive research** involves both the outlining of the nature and shape of data as well as the search for further information based on preexisting data. Since it answers factual questions like what, where, and

when, all original research involves some degree of description. These facts can be tangible and perceptible, as how John Wilkes Booth went about planning and carrying out the execution of President Lincoln, or they can be imperceptible, such as the fact that I enjoy the process of writing.

Often the description of factual information serves as a springboard to causal theories that attempt to explain how and why events happen, but other times, descriptive research represents an important contribution to knowledge by itself. For instance, in the 1870s, the archaeologist Heinrich Schliemann uncovered the ruins of ancient Troy, conclusively establishing that such a city had existed. This discovery represented a major contribution to Western civilization simply because it introduced a new understanding of something factual.

In the name of furthering knowledge, archaeologists and historians routinely attempt to describe the daily lives of peoples in times past, just as cultural anthropologists examine the ways of little-known ethnic groups in the present. Journalists frequently seek to answer important questions descriptively, like when Woodward and Bernstein found out where the money trail led in the Watergate scandal. Such research provides important answers to interesting questions without necessarily attempting to address the issues of causality that we associate with theoretical research.

Research involving statistics is often descriptive in nature as well. Simple opinion polling to determine the likely outcome of an election is descriptive research. "Toyota sells the highest percentage of foreign cars in the United States" is a descriptive sentence. Correlational research in the medical sciences often starts with little or no understanding of theory. For instance, researchers first suggested the likelihood of an association between lung cancer and smoking during the 1930s—even though they had no idea why this would be the case and could not offer a strong theoretical explanation for decades thereafter.

As a researcher begins to describe data, he or she may also derive **inferences**. An inference is what a researcher believes is occurring even though he or she may not be able to directly observe the phenomenon in question. The goal of inference is either descriptive or causal. While drawing descriptive inferences represents an effort to predict the properties of unobserved things and events, causal theory inference seeks to understand how and why some things affect other things.

Causal inferences are often built on descriptive inferences. The inference that motion distorts sound waves is a descriptive inference that can be drawn by simply standing next to railroad tracks and listening to the whistle of an approaching train. To develop a causal inference, a researcher would have to know something about the nature, frequency, and pitch of sound waves and be able to infer from this information how the distortion of sound waves influenced the sound perceived by human ears.

The discussion of descriptive research in the middle of Chapter 2 is intended in large part to help the reader distinguish the difference between descriptive and causal questions and research. Much important descriptive research has been conducted over the years in an effort to better understand the characteristics of people and past and present events, but causal research adds an additional layer of complexity by helping us understand why things happen. Nevertheless, while solid descriptive research may exist in the absence of causal understandings, causal research conducted without the underpinning of description is necessarily relegated to the realm of the abstract.

3. **Conceptualization** and **classification** represents an intermediary step between description and causal theory. Data are organized in a more rigorous manner to aid in the recognition of patterns and the development of causal inferences. It is collected and defined in broad terms, ordering it in some type of logical and understandable fashion.

Every field classifies objects, events, and phenomena in some way so that there are common frames of reference among scholars and so that causal relationships are easier to understand. Among other things, historians and paleontologists classify time periods, geographers classify regions, and biologists classify animals.

Social scientists often have a more difficult job than natural scientists, as they are called on to differentiate between different types of intangible variables such as liberal and conservative or democratic and nondemocratic. Much of the field of psychology, a social science, is built on the idea of psychological "constructs"—somewhat subjective categorizations of different mental states. The last part of Chapter 2 discusses how typologies of latent ideas are convincingly conceptualized and put into use as an organizing framework for causal theories.

4. The development of **causal theory** lies at the heart of the research process. While many excellent projects focus on the whos, whats, and whens, knowledge progresses most when a researcher is able to establish convincingly why and how something has occurred or is

occurring. While sometimes simply finding out descriptive facts is a major contribution to knowledge, most researchers want to know how and why things happen in the world as they do. Causal theories can most succinctly be thought of as a series of related cause-and-effect propositions that explain the mechanisms through which something affects something else.

Once beyond simple descriptive endeavors, research always involves causal theory in some fashion, whether a project involves the

- development of new theories,
- testing of theories, and/or
- application and refinement of theories.

As reflected in Figure 1.1, research may be thought of as always headed toward (theory building) or away from (testing and application) theoretical causal explanation.

In Chapter 3, the discussion revolves around theory building across a variety of disciplines. Within the course of the discussion, I distinguish the process deriving theory *inductively*, through the process of observation, description, and classification, from the process of deriving theory *deductively*, based on assumptions that are logical and/or mathematical in nature. Furthermore, I explore the relationship of causal theories that are based on qualitative research, which analyzes a small number of things in greater detail, with those based on quantitative research, which involves analyzing larger-scale trends in data. I provide detailed examples of major traditions that deal with each of these approaches, introducing terms such as "phenomenalism," "structuralism," and "behavioralism," and conclude with a discussion of how researchers think about the process of building their own theories.

5. **Models** and **hypotheses** are created to simplify theories and help point the way toward the process of verifying the propositions of the theory.

Models are simplified versions of the whole or parts of a theory. While causal theories entail a nuanced examination of why things happen, models usually just display the relationships between the variables described in a theory. Since they represent the essential features of theories, models aid in the formulation of concise and testable hypotheses. The efforts of researchers to develop testable models are central to quantitative efforts in the natural and social sciences.

Hypotheses are best understood as serving a specific role in research; namely, bridging the propositions of "abstract" theories and models to the expected empirical implications of those theories and models. Researchers use hypotheses to point the way to future analysis by suggesting what relationship should exist between variables that have already been rigorously examined and specified.

I examine models and hypotheses in the first part of Chapter 4. Throughout the whole chapter, I identify the steps that a researcher takes in preparing to test quantitatively oriented theories through different types of empirical analysis. Models and hypotheses are important steps in framing the testing process, but as discussed next, access to quantifiable data, which can be measured or created observationally or experimentally, is generally required as well.

6. **Operationalization** and **experimentation** are two methods of obtaining quantifiable data that can be used for statistical analysis. *Operationalization* is a term more common in the social sciences than the natural sciences. It involves efforts to measure intangible concepts quantitatively. *Experimentation* involves the deliberate manipulation of a controlled environment by a researcher to create data.

Not all data need to be transformed or "made" through experimentation. Some types of data, such as temperature or polling data, are collected in quantified form in the first place. In the absence of such naturally occurring quantitative data, a researcher might embark on the task of transforming latent, difficult-to-measure concepts into empirically measurable variables through the process of operationalization. The process of operationalization flows from the conceptualization and classification of data described in Step 3. Concepts can be ordered qualitatively and still be useful for the formulation of causal theory. However, if a researcher is investigating statistical patterns, concepts must be quantified to be useful in analysis.

The need to make concepts operational exists primarily in the social sciences, where phenomena are often not naturally quantified. Examples include concepts such as "IQ" and "power." To quantify such concepts, social scientists find related empirical referents such as test scores or size of GDP (gross domestic product). The quality of a research project often depends on how "validly," "reliably," and "precisely" information is quantified. I will discuss each of these terms at length in the middle of Chapter 4.

Unfortunately, the operationalization of intangible concepts is an inexact process. There is always room for debate about whether something was measured validly. This is a challenge that tends to face social scientists more than natural scientists, who generally employ data that are directly quantifiable through observation or experimentation.

Classic experimental techniques, on the other hand, represent the "gold standard" when it comes to the collection or creation of quantifiable data that are most appropriate for statistical testing. The reasons that experimentally derived data are often superior to observationally derived data for the purposes of testing theory are a bit complex and discussed further in the final parts of Chapter 4.

Unfortunately, not every research question is amenable to experimentation, either because of the nature of the question, the resources available to investigate the question, or the ethics involved in conducting experiments on, for example, human subjects. Thus, especially in the social sciences, experimentation is often a luxury that is out of reach for many research projects.

7. *Hypothesis testing* is conducted to determine whether, and to what degree, empirical evidence exists to support causal hypotheses. Most testing procedures help determine whether a nonrandom trend exists in data that are analyzed. This nonrandomness suggests that a relationship exists among the variables being tested. In other cases, **critical tests** examine presumed universal phenomenon and ascertain, in one-shot "experiments," whether empirical observations confirm or disconfirm whether those phenomena operate as theorized.

Statistical tests that are used to assess hypotheses differ from "descriptive statistics" in that they are designed to assess whether large sets of data support hypotheses derived from causal theory. The methods available for statistical testing are numerous and fill entire textbooks. What they all have in common, however, is the effort to ascertain the probability that patterns of data exist that provide evidence of the causal linkages posited in a researcher's theory. If a relationship is found, then statistical tests also provide answers concerning the magnitude to which independent variables affect dependent variables. Of course, if no pattern exists, that is, if statistical evidence suggests that patterns within data cannot be sufficiently differentiated from random patterns of numbers, then hypotheses must be abandoned and a theory reexamined in part or whole.[2]

Critical tests are nonstatistical in nature but can still be used to assess hypotheses. These tests, which are most associated with the natural sciences, examine specific phenomena that are presumed to reflect universal laws. This differs from the statistical testing of hypotheses, which examines trends in data rather than particular events, and does not purport to necessarily analyze universal trends. Critical testing can be summed up best as "we would expect to see" this happen if "this theory is correct." I briefly examine such critical tests in Chapter 5 before turning to a discussion of some of the basic concepts used in statistical hypothesis testing and providing a summary of some of the more common statistical methods employed by researchers.

8. **Applied theory/applied theoretical research** seeks to learn how theories might be fruitfully utilized to understand actual events. Unless research is conducted simply for "knowledge's sake," the knowledge gained from research is presumably applied to help understand real-world problems. At the same time, examining the real world helps us understand and refine theory better.

The discussion in Chapter 6 reveals how researchers use theories to achieve practical understandings of the past, present, and even future world through the use of scholarly methods such as "structured-focused" analysis and simulations. Ultimately, the utility of good theories lies in the fact that they provide the framework for understanding how things happened historically and how events might be understood today, and they can provide the lens through which predictions about the future might be made.

9. Chapter 6 also contains an exploration of more informal approaches to theoretical learning and application. The applied **"trial-and-error" approach**

---

2. As a last note about statistics, it is important to note, as presented in the model, the unidirectionality of the arrow tying together the movement from hypothesis to hypothesis testing. If a hypothesis is tested and not confirmed (or, technically, the "null hypothesis" is confirmed), it is necessary to reexamine the theoretical bases of the hypothesis, formulate a different hypothesis based on an improved understanding of the phenomenon, and collect new data with which to test the hypothesis. It is generally not appropriate to simply test and retest similar hypotheses with slightly different variables over and over again in the hope of obtaining a positive result. This is known as "data mining." For the purposes of hypothesis testing, data mining is likely to lead to a false-positive error (or Type 1 error) that will be interpreted and reported as confirmation of some element of a theory.

to knowledge reflects how real businesses and organizations function. **Theoretical refinement** and application alternate with one another in a search for "best practices." Sometimes, the process takes place as *praxis*—an attempt to put theoretical ideas into practice in the field. Other times, the approach is more passive and top-down, with a researcher observing how his or her ideas seem to illustrate what is already happening.

A researcher's theory might suggest that the world works one way and come to find that reality suggests otherwise. Confronted with a different version of causality than his or her theory presents, an author must either alter his or her understanding of theory or his or her understanding of reality. As theory and perception converge, theories become more credible and reality more decipherable.

10. The final step of research discussed in Chapter 6 involves theoretical refinement. Researchers and academics will always have jobs, because the overarching process of research is cyclical and never-ending. Few theories posited about natural and social relations turn out to be complete, universal, or display clockwork precision. The process of building on preexisting knowledge and refining the research of one's predecessors or one's own work lies at the heart of the collective effort to understand how things work. As the fruits of research are applied and understood in "real-word" contexts, researchers learn more about what they do not know and how to proceed with a different set of theoretical assumptions.

Every iteration of the research cycle can provide a greater understanding of the world. Without a firm understanding of process of research, however, our contributions as researchers will be diminished or, worse, lead future researchers to build their projects on foundations we constructed on sand.

Conclusion

In this chapter, I have laid out the basic framework for conducting research. Very few, if any, projects entail all of the steps set in Figure 1.1. However, by thinking of research as a unified whole, it is easier to visualize exactly why researchers are engaged in the particular tasks they undertake for specific projects.

In the chapters that follow, I break down Figure 1.1 into several different larger processes. The first area, which I discuss in Chapter 2, involves the effort to find, describe, and organize information (Steps 1 to 3). The second process discussed in Chapter 3 is that of theory building (Step 4). In Chapter 4 (Steps 5 and 6), I look at how researchers bridge the gap between theory and empirical testing when they conduct quantitative research. Chapter 5 is about the methods used to test whether or not causal theories are likely to be correct or not (Step 7). In Chapter 6, I discuss how researchers grapple with causal theories and their relation to the "real world" and argue that theories can inform researchers about reality, while the empirical world points the way to more refined theoretical understandings.

Each of the steps and chapters should be thought of in terms of its relationship to causal theory. Unless they are purely descriptive in nature, research projects always involve moving "toward" the creation of causal theories through the processes of inductive or deductive theory building or "away" from these theories when they are empirically tested or applied in framing and understanding events in the "real world." As such, the book is divided into three further parts, the first describing how theories are derived (Chapters 2 and 3), the second explaining how theories are empirically verified (Chapters 4 and 5), and the final section (Chapter 6) describing how theories are applied.

DISCUSSION QUESTIONS

1.1 Look at the following types of research activities. Which one do you think can best be described as (a) theory building, (b) theory testing, and (c) theory application. Why?

Using a mathematical electoral model to predict who will win an election.

Conducting an experiment and analyzing the results to determine whether a medicine improves the health of one group of people over another.

Interviewing policymakers to better understand how decisions were made in a crisis.

1.2 Look through periodicals or browse the Internet and find a news article that interests you. Think of a research question that involves the event being described and why something happened or happens. Now think of three different factors that would be worthy of investigating as potential factors explaining the outcomes described in the article you found.

PART II

Getting to Causal Theory

2

Finding and Organizing Information

Overview

This chapter covers a range of topics related to the observation and collection of data. It discusses three major sources of "observable" information: (1) first-hand observation; (2) "mediated" information taken from third-party sources such as TV, radio, and print; and (3) data collected through interviews and surveys. The discussion divides each major source of data into qualitative or quantitative types of data collection. The middle portions of the chapter differentiate descriptive projects from those involving causal research. Finally, the discussion concludes with issues of classification and definition.

Introduction

One of the most difficult parts in research is simply getting started. You usually can't get something from nothing, and the same applies to the start of the research process. Research questions do not simply pop out of thin air into a researcher's brain. A suitable research question might originate from a researcher's background knowledge of a subject, a process of **literature review**,[1] or even just informal and intuitive observation of the world. Some researchers may know exactly what they want to know at the outset of a project, but just as often, research begins on a more tentative note.

---

1. An expanded discussion of literature reviews is provided in an appendix at the end of this chapter.

Once a research question, even a tentative one, has been posed, the first steps of research involve seeking out and organizing information. Along the way, a researcher might alter or refine his or her research question, pursuing new and interesting leads as more information becomes available. The earliest, exploratory steps in research are the "messiest," as researchers attempt to pull out and organize data from the chaotic ether around them and to better understand what is happening and what yet needs to be learned.

Data represent the human interpretation of observed information. Data are "created" through the senses and intellect of researchers attempting to make sense of hitherto undiscovered facts. In this chapter, I focus on the process of collecting data through observation, making sense of that data through descriptive analysis, and the categorization of data for the purposes of theoretical development.

There are two main ways in which a researcher collects data. One way is through the process of formal experimentation, which is designed to create information where none had previously existed. For many fields, especially in the natural sciences but also in social science fields such as psychology, this is one of the main methods of collecting information about the world. I will address experimental data collection in Chapter 4.

The other way data are extracted from the environment is through comparatively more hands-off types of observation. When a researcher collects observational data, he or she is not engaging in the types of strict environmental or subject manipulation that occurs in experiments. Rather, the researcher is usually seeking out and discovering unaltered "raw" information. The beginning of the discussion in this chapter concerns the different ways in which researchers go about gathering information that they will later organize and analyze.

Observation

The term *observation* can be defined broadly or more narrowly. In the narrow sense, it can mean actually witnessing an event or process take place. Henceforth, I will refer to the process of witnessing events firsthand as "first-person observation."

In a broader sense, however, observation involves the process of seeking out and retrieving data through a variety of means and media. Observational data collection can be categorized in three ways: (1) being somewhere and collecting information through "first-person observation,"

(2) asking people about their viewpoints through interviews and surveys, and (3) obtaining information from different media sources.

Whatever method a researcher uses to collect data, it is also helpful to think about data collection as proceeding either qualitatively or quantitatively. Although these terms are fleshed out further in Chapter 3, suffice it to say, for now, that the quantitative collection and analysis of data focus on large amounts of numerical information. Qualitative data, on the other hand, involves primary source information that is not quantified or quantifiable. Each of the sections on the three types of "observation" is thus further divided into quantitative and qualitative approaches (Table 2.1).

First-Person Observation: Seeing It Yourself

Not all research projects begin with firsthand observation, but at some point, all data must either be witnessed directly by someone or reported in some way to a researcher. Even the presence of unobservable things, such as subatomic particles or prehistoric events, must be inferred from the observation of other, observable phenomena. While many research projects begin with borrowed data and borrowed theories, at some point, some person observed and recorded the original information on which subsequent research was based.

Qualitative Approaches to First-Person Observation

There are several different ways to go about designing projects that involve witnessing events "in person." Below I present a typology that

Table 2.1:   Observational Data Gathering: Qualitative and Quantitative

	Qualitative	*Quantitative*
First-person observation	Field work and "qualitative experiments"	Quantitative observational data collection (often using instruments)
Mediated data collection	Episodic record research	Running record– and content coding–type research
Opinion seeking	Most interviews, focus groups, and open-ended survey research	Large-scale polling/survey research

divides aspects of first-person observation into a series of dichotomies: direct versus indirect; structured versus unstructured; participatory versus nonparticipatory, and overt versus covert types of research.[2] These dichotomies frame most of the ways that researchers conduct first-person observational data collection (see Figure 2.1).

*Direct Versus **Indirect Observation**.* Data are obtained by (a) witnessing something as it happens or (b) observing information that might be related to another event and inferring from the available information what happened or is happening. Many kinds of first-person observation take place directly; although, with some creative "detective" work, indirect observation may yield descriptive clues as well.

In particular, the terms *accretion* and *erosion* measures are related to indirect observation. Accretion measures involve inferring information based on the accumulation of something in the observed environment; erosion measures involve the subtraction of something from that environment. One prominent accretion measure used to infer another event was the 1980 discovery by Luis and Walter Alvarez of the presence of extremely high amounts of the mineral iridium on the sedimentary layer of earth associated with the period when the dinosaurs became extinct (see, e.g., Alvarez, 1997). Since large deposits of iridium are usually only associated with massive volcanic eruptions and asteroid strikes, the discovery of the deposits indirectly linked the extinction of the dinosaurs to some catastrophic geological event at that time.

Erosion measures function similarly. While erosion might occur in the environment, human beings contribute to erosion through the wear and tear of their actions. A librarian might conclude that certain books at a library were more popular by observing which ones had looser spines, more sections underlined, or greater evidence of previously dog-eared pages.

The defining difference between direct and indirect observation is whether or not we can see something occurred or we have to infer that it is happening based on what we are seeing. An example of indirect observation in cosmology might be observations over recent years that stars wobble gravitationally as a planet circles them. Only recently have those

---

2. The categories and discussion in the following section are loosely informed by a similar discussion in Johnson and Reynolds' (2008, chap. 8) *Political Science Research Methods*, an excellent text that I have used numerous times in my own classes and which has undoubtedly conditioned my thinking on these issues to some degree.

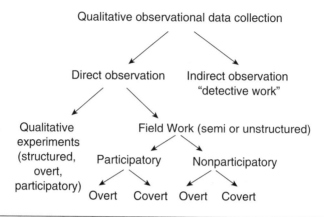

Figure 2.1:   Breakdown of qualitative observational data collection

observations become direct as more powerful telescopes have been invented that can actually view the presence of such planets.

*Structured Versus **Unstructured Observation.*** When engaging in qualitative projects, some researchers begin with more of a "game plan" than others. The more refined the initial research question, the more specific the information sought by a researcher. When a research environment is more structured, the researcher knows what information he or she seeks and looks for specific data within the setting he or she has chosen to observe. This applies also to interview settings, when the questions asked have been chosen in advance.

One type of structured (or at least semistructured) observation is what might be called a **qualitative experiment**. While this is not a widely used term among methodologists, there are important differences between qualitative experiments and the *classic experiments* that I will discuss in Chapter 4. While classic experiments involve strict procedures that are designed to validly test hypotheses, qualitative experiments are intended primarily as exercises in theory building.[3]

Qualitative experiments involve some intervention by a researcher who intends to observe as subsequent events unfold in the controlled

---

3. I distinguish the term *qualitative experiment* from quasi-experiment, a research tool that I will discuss toward the end of Chapter 4. Quasi-experiments are more structured than qualitative experiments and might be thought of as a middle ground between the design-and-then-sit-back-and-observe nature of qualitative experiments and the rigorous interventions of classic experiments.

environment he or she has created. An example in social research involved assigning two different colored shirts to two different groups of children attending a summer school program (Patterson & Bigler, 2006) and then observing, after several weeks, how children felt and reacted to other members of their "in-group" versus the "out-group." Another example was the famous (some would say infamous) "Stanford Prison Experiment" conducted by Philip Zimbardo in 1971 that involved selecting 24 student volunteers, assigning them roles as either guards or prisoners, and then observing their subsequent interaction in a makeshift prison environment (http://www.angelfire.com/or/sociologyshop/path.html). In the cases of both examples just mentioned, researchers place subjects in a structured environment and then allow events to play out in order to "see what happens."

In unstructured observation, on the other hand, the researcher knows what topic he or she wants to observe but generally does not have enough information to know in advance what the best research question might be to ask. In other words, unstructured observation is largely exploratory, at least at first. As the researcher immerses himself or herself in an environment, the topics of interest are expected to emerge as events unfold. This mirrors what Fenno (1978), in a field study on the behavior of congressional representatives, famously referred to as "soak and poke"—soaking up information while poking around for more in an unstructured fashion.

Participatory Versus *Nonparticipatory Observation.* "Participatory observation" is a phrase that every qualitative social scientist knows well, and it refers to the types of field studies that are common in areas of sociology, education studies, and anthropology, in particular. In these cases, the researcher is an active member of the environment in which he or she is studying—often a social or occupational environment. An education major, for instance, might serve as teacher's aide while observing and reporting to another audience about the experiences he or she had. A cultural anthropologist might live among the villagers of a rural ethnic group, taking part in the experiences of everyday life, to understand the interactions and perspectives of those living there.

When a researcher is actively engaged in participant observation, however, it is possible that ethical questions will arise. For instance, engaging in criminal activity while observing a group would be a clear violation of standards of scholarly integrity. In other cases, it is not simply a matter of the researcher's actions but whether or not the nature of his or her intentions has been made clear to those under observation.

When observing the natural world (i.e., things other than people), non-participation is clearly the norm. Where human beings are involved, however, nonparticipatory observation involves the researcher as a "fly-on-the-wall" who takes note of the events and activities around him or her while preserving his or her role as a detached observer. Journalists frequently engage in nonparticipatory observation as they take notes and report on events of importance without actively engaging in the process they are observing.

Overt Versus **Covert Observation***.* Unique to the social sciences is the distinction between overt and covert research. To avoid ethical complication, most scholarly research is carried out overtly—with the subjects of the research aware of the project that is taking place. In other cases within the social sciences, however, a researcher might decide that subjects who were aware of the researcher's presence might behave differently than they would otherwise. In this case, a researcher decides to wear the hat of the "undercover reporter" who immerses himself or herself in the research environment without the knowledge of those around him or her. The advantage of this is that subjects will act naturally and not react to the presence of the researcher. The disadvantage is that undercover research might be considered an invasion of privacy, even if the identities of the subjects remain confidential.

One famous covert study was Humphreys's (1975) sociological study of the characteristics of gay men frequenting public restrooms. Humphreys served, on location, as a "watch queen" charged with keeping a lookout for the authorities. He also subsequently followed the subjects to parking lots to record their license plate numbers, which he later used to track them down at their places of residence and covertly interview them about their social characteristics. Humpreys's covert study was controversial at the time and would likely not have been approved by modern **institutional review boards** that must be consulted at most modern universities before research projects involving human subjects may be conducted.

Quantitative Observational Studies and Instruments

The collection of quantitative data from the natural world is the bread and butter of the natural sciences, although examples exist in the social sciences as well. **Quantitative observational data**, numerical information recorded from the direct observation and measurement of a phenomenon, is rarely measured directly. Most quantitative observational studies rely on instruments that assist in obtaining accurate data.

Data collection assisted by instruments is most familiar to those in the natural sciences that rely on increasingly complex technologies to obtain information from the environment. Instruments are necessary when information, like temperature, is not directly measurable through the human senses. The use of intermediary instruments suggests that this type of research often dovetails with the idea of "indirect observation." A climatologist might consult thermometers for indications of global temperatures or he or she might take samples from tree rings to derive similar information. Physicists might observe the trajectories of particles smashed together, but only as represented on sophisticated computers.

As an intermediary between the observer and the phenomenon being measured, instruments may deliver accurate or inaccurate data that affect a researcher's inferences. In one famous case during the late 1980s, a team of physicists that reported success in achieving cold fusion had their findings subsequently and scandalously debunked. One contributing reason appears to have involved erroneous readings obtained from their primary measuring instrument, a calorimeter. As a fellow scientist later put it, "Tens of millions of dollars at stake, Dear Brother, because some scientist put a thermometer at one place and not another" (quoted in Brown, 1989).

One particular "instrument" that is used for collecting data is known as a "survey instrument"—which is a fancy way of saying a questionnaire used for opinion polling. These types of instruments are subject to a variety of problems that might yield questionable results as well. I examine this type of instrument later in the chapter.

Unfortunately, quantitative observational data can have major drawbacks when they are used to draw causal inferences. Apart from the propensity for measurement error, there also exists the potential for **omitted variable biases** and **simultaneity/reverse causality bias**. Omitted variables are variables that might affect a relationship but are not included in an analysis. Simultaneity/reverse causality bias, as the name suggests, occurs when there is a misinterpretation of the directionality of causal relationships.[4] Both of these problems are mitigated when data are obtained experimentally rather than observationally, a matter further discussed in Chapter 4.

---

4. Sometimes simultaneity/reverse causality bias is known simply as **endogeneity**. In statistics, however, endogeneity encompasses several types of bias including omitted variable bias, measurement problems, and simultaneity/reverse causality bias.

"Media"-ted Data Collection: Obtaining Data From the Middleman

Mediated data collection[5] suggests more distance between the empirical world and the researcher than direct first-person observation. In this type of observation, the research is making use of "raw" data that originate from others who have collected and recorded information for their own purposes or for the use of others. Sources include books, websites, TV, radio, films, newspaper articles, recordings, data sets, documents, or any other type of information compiled by another person. The focus is on primary rather than secondary sources. The difference between the two is that **primary sources** represent raw, uninterpreted data, while **secondary sources** involve research projects in which an author has already interpreted data to develop his or her own theories.

Qualitative Mediated Observation: Episodic Records

Sources of data used for qualitative projects tend to differ from those used for quantitative ones. Qualitative research generally makes use of contextual **episodic records** like personal diaries, letters, government memos, speeches, journalistic accounts, or other information that has originated from individuals who have been recording information about particular events and circumstances. It often takes a lot of time and energy to find and obtain these sources, although their sometimes obscure nature often leads to unique and important research contributions. Historians, in particular, are associated with the use of these primary sources with the goal of developing descriptive and qualitative theories. However, throughout the humanities and social sciences the use of qualitative document analysis is common.

Quantitative Mediated Observation: Running Records and Content Analysis

Quantitative research often makes use of what has been termed **running records** (Johnson & Reynolds, 2008; Lee, 2000). Running records are composed of data that are intentionally collected and compiled for future

---

5. The term *mediated data collection* is not a term that is generally used when discussing methodology. I have not found, however, another term that adequately describes what I am discussing, namely, the use of intermediary sources as a source of observational data early in the research process.

analysis. Financial and medical records are good examples as are voting records, economic data, records of births and deaths, and any social or natural science data set. Such materials are ready-made for quantitative observation and future analysis. In general, it is considered important scientific practice to make available for public use any data that have been collected and organized for the use of a completed research project.

Oftentimes, social scientists seek to quantify data that are found in "qualitative sources," such as newspaper articles or visual media. In a process known simply as **content analysis**, researchers code and compile counts of key words, phrases, or concepts from a sample of such sources. The term connotes research conducted in fields that study human communication, but there is no reason that the term cannot be extended to any similar process that involves quantitatively coding data derived from any type of written or oral material. Thus, the goal of content analysis often involves an analysis of either media coverage itself or how individuals or groups have expressed themselves through the media, such as how many acts of violence occur in a given hour of prime-time television or how many times politicians refers to "social welfare" in their speeches.

Sometimes the procedures used to code data are somewhat subjective in nature. This is especially true if a researcher's project involves coding intangible concepts and ideas that different researchers might interpret differently. The best way to overcome this problem is to be as specific as possible about the coding criteria used for inclusion or exclusion, without being so specific as to lose sight of what is being investigated. In cases where different researchers might reach different conclusions, statistics (there are several that might be used) measuring **intercoder reliability** compare the results of different researchers who coded the same material.

Content analysis is one of the most common methods used in the social sciences. The uses are incredibly varied, from determining strategies people use to lie (Aldert, Edward, & Bull, 2001) to newspaper coverage of the poor (Rose & Baumgartner, 2013) to how people portray themselves in personal ads (Lun, Mesquita, & Smith, 2011). In one amusing study that gained national attention, Conway, Grabe, and Grieves (2007) analyze the rhetoric used by political pundit Bill O'Reilly and find, among other things, that the host called people or groups derogatory names an average of once every 6.8 seconds in the opening segments of his show. There are literally thousands of studies such as these that use content analysis across every field in the social sciences.

Opinion Seeking: Interviews and Polling/Surveys

Along with first-person observation and mediated collection, interviews and surveys represent a third method of data collection. In these cases, the point is not to seek out information to study firsthand or through the media but, rather, to ask others about their personal characteristics, opinions, and perspectives. As with other forms of observation and data collection, the "ask others" approaches can be divided into more qualitative data collection and more quantitative data collection. Interviews are more often than not conducted for qualitative purposes, while survey, or polling, data are collected primarily for quantitative purposes.

Qualitative Opinion Seeking: Interviews

There exists a continuum of interviewing styles and purposes that are in between those that are highly structured and those that are considered unstructured interviews, with different degrees of "semistructured" interviews occupying the middle ground and combining techniques of both. The purposes of structured interviews on one side of the interview spectrum and the purposes of unstructured interviews on the other can be quite different and will be discussed below. What ultimately sets interviewing in general apart from the polling/survey research described in the next section is that interviews are ultimately focused on the characteristics and opinions of the interviewees themselves, while opinion polling is about using participant feedback as a method of gauging descriptive trends in larger populations.

Since they tend to be focused on individuals and nonrepresentative small groups, it is best to think of interviewing as a primarily qualitative methodology. There are, however, quantitative aspects to structured interviews. Structured interviews involve a specific, preset group of questions that lend themselves to numerical coding applications similar to those of content analysis. Unlike content analysis of documents or media that usually focuses on describing general data trends, the point of a structured interview is normally to use preexisting research and standards to categorize and label characteristics of particular individuals, as a psychologist might do with a patient or the U.S. Office of Personnel Management does for some would-be government workers.[6]

---

6. The U.S. Government's Office of Personnel Management (2008) has posted an interesting book on their structured interviewing methods at https://apps.opm.gov/ADT/ContentFiles/SIGuide09.08.08.pdf.

Unlike structured interviews, unstructured interviews are more natu-rally conversational in nature. Any preprepared questions eventually give way to a more free-flowing discussion. While many researchers in this tradition have eschewed the idea of preestablished interviewing proce-dures (see, e.g., the historical discussion found in Fontana & Frey, 1994, pp. 362–366), those interviewing techniques that do exist describe how an interviewer can convey an encouraging, empathic, and nonjudgmental attitude verbally and nonverbally, spatially, and through the choice of set-ting. As opposed to largely unstructured interviews, semistructured inter-views usually involve a larger degree of advanced preparation that is still coupled with a willingness to depart from the script and follow up interesting lines of inquiry where required.

Like many other qualitative undertakings, less structured interviews are inappropriately judged by standards like "validity" and "reliability." This makes the methodology of interviewing a bit "fast and loose" with respect to any strict methodology. While many qualitative scholars eschew strict "techniques," one area explored by qualitative methodolo-gists involves for eliciting as much information from a subject as possible. The art of judicious "probing" to obtain more information from a subject is explored by numerous authors (e.g., Camino, Zelden, & Payne-Jackson, 1995; Schmidt & Conaway, 1998). Some, such as Bernard (2002, p. 217), even suggest using "silent probing" as a way of eliciting information by knowing when not to speak! Authors such as Bell (1993) offer extensive checklists involving other techniques and logistical issues that interview-ers can expect to face.

Unstructured (and some semistructured) interviews usually focus more on obtaining information related to interpretations and perspectives than descriptive data. As opposed to journalists, who are more likely to engage in investigative "what happened?"–type interviews, academics tend to be more interested in understanding how a subject perceives his or her environment and his or her role in it. As such, less structured types of interviewing are common to the very qualitative traditions of *phenome-nology* and **ethnography** described in Chapter 3.

Interviews do not always take place with individuals. Groups of peo-ple might be interviewed as well. Oftentimes, when a group is inter-viewed for a specific purpose, such as to garner perspectives and reactions to events such as political discussions or movie screenings, the group is known as a **focus group**. The selection of a focus group does not follow strict methodological dictates, and thus, it cannot be considered a valid representation of larger public opinion. Nevertheless, such groups can provide a range of perspectives on subject matters of interest. Focus groups, like interviews, can also provide ideas and feedback that lend themselves to the construction of quantitative polling surveys meant to gauge broader opinion.

Quantitative Opinion Seeking: Surveys/Polling[7]

Polling is a valuable tool for social scientists. To obtain information through polling, social scientists devise **survey instruments**. Survey instruments, or "questionnaires," are designed to measure more general public opinion as closely as possible. Unlike interviews, the goal of polling is not to obtain a complex look at individual perceptions. Rather, the goal is to collect enough information to accurately estimate how large groups of people would respond to a series of simple questions.

Valid polling must address two issues. The first involves seeking the best **sample** of observations that will reflect the larger **population** that the sample is meant to represent. Second, the survey instrument itself needs to be carefully designed so that survey responses remain as unclouded by biases and misunderstandings as possible. I discuss below some of the basic issues associated with each step of the process.

Samples and Strategies in Polling Research

The search for population subsets, or samples, that accurately reflect general opinion is the most important step that separates polling/survey research from large-scale interviewing. Sometimes surveys can be taken of an entire population—all employees at a given business, for instance. Such a "sample" is defined as a **census**.

For a census, sampling is unproblematic because the sample and the population are the same. However, much of the time, the entire population of interest would be too difficult and costly to survey. In these cases, the goal of the researcher is to collect responses from a subset of individuals

---

7. Polls and surveys are essentially the same thing, only polls tend to be shorter, "one-question" types of surveys, whereas traditional surveys are more associated with longer sets of questionnaires. The term *survey research* is often used to describe any research that is quantitative and observational in nature, rather than simply that involving the solicitation of people's opinions. To avoid confusion, I tend to use the word "polling" where possible to emphasize that the research involves people. Nevertheless, whether a short poll or a long survey, the methodological issues remain the same.

(a sample) from the larger group that would best (most validly) represent the views of the group as a whole.

The basic principle of representative sampling is that every unit from a population has the same chance of being selected as a research participant as any other. **Probabilistic sampling** of this kind must entail some element of random selection of participants, whereas **nonprobabilistic sampling** may entail direct, nonrandom selection of subjects by the researcher. Nonprobabilistic sampling techniques, however, cannot create a sample that would be expected to accurately represent general opinion. Such techniques include **convenience sampling**, which implies exactly as it sounds that subjects are chosen based on ease of accessibility; **quota sampling**, which deliberately attempts to select a range of opinions, but not randomly; and **snowball sampling**, which seeks out subjects through social or career networks. All of these nonprobabilistic approaches should be thought of as ways of choosing subjects for group interviews and focus groups rather than as a way to achieve representativeness.

Probabilistic sampling, however, will yield samples that, if selected over and over again, would reflect something close to the average responses of the larger group that such samples are selected to represent. The most straightforward of the probabilistic techniques is known as **simple random sampling**. Random sampling simply entails selecting subjects from a population completely randomly for purposes of **survey research**. This is a valid way of approaching data collection such that it maximizes the chances of measuring the underlying concept, general opinion.

How reliably and precisely a survey of a given sample is expected to measure the underlying "true" population's opinions is a different story. Every randomly selected sample will be different from one another— some will yield responses that are more representative, some less so. How likely a given random sample is to yield representative answers largely depends on (a) the size of the sample and (b) the degree that different observational values are "spread out" in a population (i.e., population variance).

As with any data, trends become more evident through polling when the sample size is larger. Although people might give different answers, patterns of more-common and less-common answers emerge as more people are surveyed. As more data are gathered, sample answers will converge more and more on the "true opinion" of the population from which the participants were drawn—a phenomenon related to the *law of large numbers*, which will be discussed further in Chapter 4. In short, within the bounds of time and logistic feasibility, more information is always better than less information.[8]

The second factor in assessing how close sample responses are likely to be to true popular opinion involves how spread out the distribution of responses is. This is more intuitive if we think of an example: Individuals are asked to respond to the question "How tall are you?" If most people were of different heights, it would be hard to narrow down the average height of the people in the population without a relatively large sample size. If more people were clustered around the average in a **bell curve** shape (aka a **normal distribution**[9]), however, it is more likely that any individual's height chosen at random would be closer to the average than the situation when the distribution of heights is more spread out. In other words, a random person chosen in a sample with smaller variance would be more likely "typical" of the population than a person chosen when people's heights were more spread out. Taken together, the size of a sample and its variance can be used to calculate a **sample error**, which suggests how close a researcher's sample data is likely to reflect the characteristics of a population.

When it comes to surveying people, one "problem" is that no one can be forced to participate. Thus, samples involving people are never truly random. In addition, the likelihood that someone will participate in a survey is often correlated with the answers they would tend to give on a questionnaire. For instance, if a researcher paid people $5 on the street to take a survey about whether or not enough social support programs exist in your town, the researcher would likely obtain a sample with a disproportionate number of people who are in greater need of a couple of dollars, a fact which might correlate with support of social support programs. Differing **response rates** among particular groups of people leads to **selection bias**, the term for the problem that arises when the

---

8. While more information is always better in principle, the representativeness of samples increases with diminishing returns as more subjects participate. For instance, the (95%) **margin of error** of a poll, a statistic derived from the number of participants in the poll and the variability of responses, decreases from 4.4% for a sample of 500 in a "large population with evenly split opinions" to 3.1% for a sample of 1,000 obtained from the same population. However, moving from a sample size of 1,000 to 1,500 only decreases the margin of error from 3.1% to 2.5%.

9. Any *distribution* in statistics indicates the values of a variable and the frequency, or probability, in which those values occur.

composition of a sample is a determining factor for the outcome and conclusions of the research being conducted.

Fortunately, statisticians have developed a way to sample individuals for survey research that can help mitigate both random sample error and selection bias. **Stratified sampling** conducts sampling based on preexisting information that is available to the researcher. If such preexisting information exists and is largely correct (two big "ifs"!), then a researcher can often improve both the precision and validity of his or her survey procedures.

For example, let's say a researcher suspected that a different percentage of men than women will answer a survey question in a particular way. In the United States, we know from census data that men make up about 49% of the population and women make up about 51% of the population. If we randomly sampled 100 people for our survey and, by random chance, 52% of those people turned out to be men and 48% turned out to be women, we know already that the sample is not entirely representative of the underlying population in terms of gender.

Under these conditions, using the previous existing information that we have, stratified sampling would improve on simple random sampling by first dividing men and women into different "strata" based on their relative population proportions and then randomly sampling within those strata. Our results are likely to be more precise than simple random sampling, and because people are still chosen randomly within each stratum, the research design still remains valid. The same "preexisting information" principle applies when researchers attempt to overcome differing response rate issues. If a researcher knows, for instance, that women are likely to answer the phone (or answer the door, or respond through the mail) 60% of the time and men only 40%, then stratified sampling can alleviate this bias through the intentional selection of fewer women for the survey.

As was noted, the downside of stratified sampling is that it requires accurate preexisting information to conduct. Polling organizations frequently use stratified sampling, however, to mitigate a variety of response-rate issues in areas for which preexisting information might be available—gender, income rates, cell phone usage, race, party affiliation, and so on. Sometimes the preexisting information is simply a "best guess" based on response trends that have been observed in the past. When successful, however, stratified sampling represents an improvement over simple random sampling when it comes to choosing a sample that is most likely to reflect the true opinions and characteristics of a larger population of interest.

Survey Instrument Design

While the pursuit of representative samples might separate survey research from interviewing, the importance of formulating and formatting questions in such a way that the data gathered appropriately answers the questions sought in the research is an area that both surveys and interviews share. The way in which questions are asked can have a profound effect on the way they are answered. While perfect polling research will always be elusive, there are several issues that, if a researcher keeps them in mind while conducting research, can improve the quality of the information gathered.

First, it bears mentioning that the major thrust of polling tends to involve close-ended questions; questions that require a respondent to provide answers in one of several preset categories. Open-ended questions are used on many surveys as well. These types of questions allow respondents to provide free form answers that elaborate on other survey questions or provide new thoughts and perspectives in areas not covered by the rest of the survey. Just as structured interviews may include quantitative coding, open-ended survey questions introduce a qualitative element into what is primarily quantitative research.

As far as close-ended questions are concerned, there are many issues that a researcher must consider if the answers given are to be representative of general opinion. Questions must be carefully worded to prevent the introduction of bias through leading questions or confusion through ambiguous or misleading ones. The ordering of questions must be considered so that the answer to one question does not affect the answers to other questions. Long questionnaires may lead to fatigue on the part of the subject answering the questions, which, in turn, leads to less careful consideration of what is being asked.

One of the most difficult issues of all involves respondent knowledge and ego. Unless a survey covers everyday events familiar to everyone in a given sample, there will be those who have not thought about or are unfamiliar with the subject matter being asked. Subjects often fall back on best guesses and heuristic clues in the wording of questions to avoid sounding ignorant. For instance, most surveys suggest that less than half of Americans can name their congressional representative and even fewer the representative's political affiliation. Yet many polls that ask citizens whether they view their congressional representative favorably or unfavorably find that fewer than 10% of respondents answer "no opinion." Clearly, in such cases, there is a certain gap in the nature of the question being asked and the quality of the responses provided.

Unfortunately, no matter what the issue, there is no foolproof way to overcome the problems associated with differing degrees of knowledge, interest, and ego among respondents concerning the questions being asked. As with other measures taken in designing questionnaires, the best that can be done is to design questions that take into account these factors and encourage participants to opt for choices indicating they do not know or have no opinion when that is the case.

Description

While observation involves the collection of data, the process of "description" involves the first steps in organizing and interpreting the data. The term **descriptive research** connotes an effort to understand "what is happening." While observation involves collecting information about different elements involved in the subject of study, descriptive research involves understanding the characteristics of those elements and often attempting to understand whether there is any observed interconnections between them. To use a simple analogy, observation might involve choosing a subject and collecting the necessary art supplies, while description would involve actually painting the picture.

The term *descriptive research* is also important in terms of what it does not represent. By itself, descriptive research is not causal research. Descriptive research does not explore how or why things happen as they do. Descriptive research might be a building block in the construction of causal theories but does not itself represent an attempt to explore causality.

Figure 2.2 gives examples of the types of questions that might be asked, depending on whether or not a research project's goal is descriptive or causal. Both descriptive and causal research might ask questions that are more contextual, or qualitative, or more quantitative[10] in nature. It should be noted from the examples, however, that it is almost always the case that research into causality requires descriptive information about what happened before an investigation of why something happened can proceed.

Descriptive studies often take the form of "atheoretical" (noncausal) case studies. A researcher studies a particular situation to understand what is actually happening. In a sense, this is what a journalist often does, leaving

10. I will discuss the matter of "qualitative" versus "quantitative" research in greater depth in Chapter 3. For now, suffice it to say that qualitative research involves investigating a small number of things in particular contexts, while quantitative research involves examining large numbers of things.

	Descriptive	Causal
Qualitative	How has life changed in a village as globalization has progressed?	Why has globalization affected the inhabitants of the village as it has?
Quantitative	Do most Americans support health care reform?	How and why is American support for health care reform different from that of other countries?

Figure 2.2:   Descriptive versus causal research questions

causal interpretation for the editorial page. It is also the main type of information reported in Wikipedia articles and other similar reference materials. Academics engage in this type of research as well, although often as an precursor to further research into cause-and-effect relationships.

Descriptive studies build on both direct and indirect types of observation. Building on direct observation, description represents a comprehensive, contextual recounting of events. Oftentimes, however, description is indirect and must draw on observer inferences to fill in the factual blanks. Descriptive inference involves suggesting a factual answer to questions (who, what, where, and when) even if those facts are not directly observed.

Lawyers engage in battles over descriptive inferences when they attempt to establish the circumstances of a crime. They present preexisting data and then attempt to persuade juries that the evidence supports a particular version of events that neither the jury nor the lawyer has witnessed. Persuasive arguments presumably rely on more than rhetoric. They rely on the weight of evidence pointing to a particular factual conclusion that is drawn from more readily observable information. Court proceedings ultimately represent a debate about the appropriate interpretation of descriptive inferences.

The divide between descriptive versus causal research can be thought of as another important dimension of research similar to that of the difference between qualitative versus quantitative research. Table 2.2 provides examples of types of professions that we might associate with each "dimension" of research.

Like observation, descriptive research may be pursued more qualitatively or quantitatively. The contextual examination of a case or a small number of cases is best thought of as qualitative description. Quantitative description often employs **descriptive statistics**—measurements that

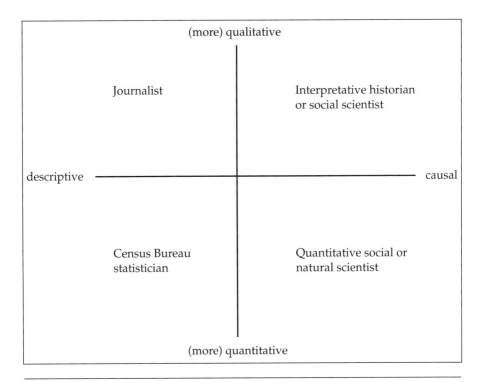

Table 2.2:   Examples of professions by research "dimension"

describe the distribution of measured data.[11] Descriptive statistics differ from **inferential statistics**, are often used to assess causal relationships, and are discussed in further depth in Chapter 5.

A descriptive statistic that examines the properties of a particular variable is known as a **univariate statistic**. Most people have some passing familiarity with univariate statistics, which examine characteristics such as mean value, median value, standard deviation, and variance. These statistics improve on simple observation by providing a better idea of the contours of the raw data that have been collected.

Other types of descriptive statistics examine the relationship of variables to one another without specifying causal relationships. **Bivariate statistics** are used to understand relationships between two variables.

---

11. If, however, characteristics of a population are estimated from a sample, such as is the case with opinion polling, the estimates are (univariate) inferential statistics. Basically, the defining difference between descriptive and inferential statistics is that descriptive statistics convey exact information about a sample, while inferential statistics represent probabilistic estimates based on sample information.

Commonly utilized **correlation analysis**, for instance, examines the strength and direction of the linear relationship between (usually two) variables. The most commonly used correlation statistic is "Pearson's product-moment correlation coefficient," often denoted with an "r." This statistic varies from −1 to 1, with 0 denoting no correlation, and −1 and 1 indicating a perfect linear relationship. The sign of the correlation coefficient denotes the direction of the relationship, either positive or negative. Positive correlations indicate that variables tend to either increase or decrease in tandem with one another. Negative correlations indicate an inverse relationship, as one variable increases the other tends to decrease.

The value of the correlation is not an actual unit, but a ratio between how much the variables move in tandem (covariance) over how much they vary from their means individually (standard deviation). Since correlation statistics are not reported in standard units, a researcher has to get somewhat "of a feel" for what a strong or weak correlation is, given the subject matter being studied. Relations in the natural sciences, for instance, demand a higher degree of correlation to be convincing than the more imprecise relationships studied in most social sciences.

Another way of interpreting an "r" value is to multiply it by itself. The **r-squared (r^2) values** represent the total percentage of the movement in the variables that can be explained by one another. For instance, Cohen (1981) studies student evaluation scores received by graduate students teaching similar course sections and finds they correlate with final testing scores in each section at $r = .43$. Multiplying .43 by itself yields and r-squared value of about .185. This indicates that only about 18.5% of the variation in the teaching evaluation scores is reflected in the variation of the test scores (and vice versa).

Correlational analysis also aids in grouping similar variables together. Sometimes highly correlated variables are measuring something similar. If several variables seem to be measuring the same thing, a researcher might group them together in an overarching *concept* or **construct** that incorporates all of them.

The idea of building constructs brings us to the final section on classification and conceptualization. To build theories, one must classify data in some fashion. This includes constructing variables and grouping similar variables together in a sensible fashion. This process does not necessarily mean that information has to exist in a preexisting quantified form. It simply suggests that to proceed with causal theory building at a later point, one must bring a certain order out of the chaos of information that one obtains from simply observing the world. The process of classification and conceptualization occurs concurrently with, and flows from, efforts to observe and describe events.

Classification and Conceptualization

As I had suggested in the research model (Figure 1.1), there is an intermediate step between description and the development of causal theory. When the main point of research is descriptive, rather than causal, a researcher may focus more on developing a holistic, big picture of the information he or she has collected without engaging in more rigorous attempts to categorize different observed phenomenon. However, when the end goal of research is the development of theory, it is usually important to categorize and organize descriptive information such that observations are clearly defined so that similar phenomena are placed together in similar groupings.

Engaging conceptual terminology is, in general, an important scholarly and pedagogical undertaking. Sometimes the search for convincing and justifiable definitions of unclear concepts is a project unto itself, especially among philosophers. Instructors employing the "Socratic Method" in class, for instance, attempt to get students to engage in abstract concepts like "justice" in a manner that refines their thinking about such terms that are often taken for granted.

Definitional clarity is not enough, however. Information that is collected must be sensibly organized to draw causal linkages between the different factors being examined. The pivotal role that organization and definition plays is explained succinctly by Jones (1986, p. 82), who writes "Explanation requires comparison; comparison requires classification; classification requires the definition of those facts to be classified, compared, and ultimately explained."

Classification involves grouping together similar things, while **conceptualization** involves defining more precisely what those things are and what elements constitute them. Classification is generally associated with the term **taxonomy**, while conceptualization is associated with the term **typology**. Bailey (1994, p. v) suggests a helpful distinction between the two terms by asserting that a taxonomy creation is best understood as an effort to organize tangible and empirical data, while a typology creation represents an effort to clarify an intangible phenomenon.

Since data are often more directly observable in the natural sciences, the creation of taxonomies, rather than more social science–oriented typologies, is the more common method of organizing data. The most well-known example of taxonomy is in the biological sciences, where plants, animals, and other organisms are grouped into categories based on their similarities. However, the creation of taxonomy can involve the categorization of any tangible data. Another famous example from the natural sciences was the controversial 2006 decision made by the International Astronomical Association to reclassify the planets in such a way as to exclude Pluto. Although the decisions involving what dividing lines to use in taxonomies might sometimes become the subject of debate, the values assigned to each category are usually less subjective than the process of conceptualizing intangible social science variables.

The creation of typologies is more complicated because concepts are inherently "latent," that is, hidden, or not directly observable. More so than taxonomies, they are somewhat subjective—there are no definitively right or wrong definitions of concepts even if some definitions are more convincing than others. Nevertheless, to build a working typography, some type of workable definition must be asserted so that a researcher can define when a variable is something and when it is not. To define a concept (or "construct"), it must be clearly understood in terms of its constituent parts.

Take, for example, the classic case of defining democracy. If a political researcher is going to ask questions about how democracies come about or how democracies differ from other types of governments in their performance and behavior, then one of the first tasks of the researcher will be to define, as specifically as possible, what a democratic government actually is. Since voting is not, by itself, a sufficient factor by most definitions in labeling a country a democracy (most nondemocratic countries conduct some type of voting procedure), the researcher would have to make a case for what specific factors would also be needed to be included in a definition.

One way in which concepts are clarified is through the process of **conceptual mapping**. Informal conceptual maps are used in a variety of fields as an aid in "brainstorming" ideas that are related to a concept. More formal conceptual maps, however, are sometimes used to help researchers rigorously define and link the different elements of concepts together.

A formal conceptual map is generally present as an inverted "tree" (see, e.g., Figure 2.3). The main concept is presented at the top of the diagram, which is then subdivided into branches representing constituent subconcepts. These subconcepts themselves are sometimes further broken down as well (and so on). If later quantitative analysis is going to be performed, the final "leaves" of the tree should be terms that are measurable in some way.

The guiding principle of conceptualization is that each concept should be broken down into elements that are (a) mutually exclusive, (b) exhaustive (Bailey, 1994, p. 7), (c) do not involve conflating inappropriate

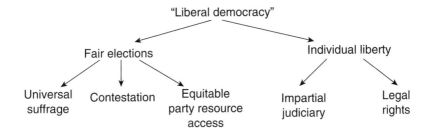

Figure 2.3:   Example of a "conceptual map"

subcategories (Munck & Verkuilen, 2002, p. 14), and (d) relevant to the main concept. Mutual exclusivity means that the subconcepts into which the main concept is broken should not repeat themselves. Such redundancy would occur when the subconcepts reflect similar attributes, in whole or part, in such a way that it is difficult to distinguish the elements from one another.

In addition to avoiding redundancy, a concept should be broken down exhaustively. The attributes, or subconcepts, that are used to describe the main concept should define that concept in its totality, not simply some aspects of it.

The issue of conflation arises when dissimilar elements are lumped together under a common attribute or miscategorized under one attribute when they would more appropriately belong under another. This becomes a particular problem as conceptualization becomes more complex.

Last, the elements, or subconcepts, that are theorized to make up the main concept should be relevant. While qualitative scholars might argue about which subconcepts are appropriate for inclusion in the conceptualization of a term, there are sometimes quantitative methods available that help researchers decide which elements seem to fit best with other elements. I will discuss methods such as interitem correlation and factor analysis in Chapter 5.

Not all concepts are diagrammed as trees—although such a visual aid is often helpful. Oftentimes the idea of conceptualizing important terms is as simple as identifying the term's necessary attributes. Avoiding conceptual ambiguity, however, is important to all research, qualitative and quantitative.

Combining the subconcepts that make up the main construct is often a difficult task. Munck and Verkuilen (2002, p. 28), for instance, find fault with the Freedom House Index, which contains composite variables that purport to measure the concept of relative "freedom" in all countries across the globe. The Freedom House Index involves over two dozen attributes that are assessed in determining each country's level of "freedom." When so many elements come into play, it is very difficult to maintain the mutual exclusivity of each one, leading a degree of redundancy and conflation that calls the whole measurement system into question.

Equally challenging is the question of how the attributes of a concept are thought to fit together. It is one thing to suggest that democracy involves political inclusiveness and elections, but what are the relationships among the elements? Is one more important than the other? If so, to what degree? Must all the elements exist for the concept to be present? Such questions exist anytime a composite variable is created out of a combination of subconcepts.

If the goal is to simply aid in qualitative theory building, a researcher may not have to specify and measure different elements of a concept in detail. However, if the purpose of a research project is to empirically assess the role played by a concept in a causal relationship, then how the subconcepts are measured and pieced together becomes essential to the research process. In Chapter 4, I will pick up again with the discussion of conceptionalization and describe how concepts can be *operationalized* by assigning numerical values to them.

"Grounding" Theory

Much of what I have described in this chapter relates to the somewhat nebulous idea of "grounding" theory. Glaser and Strauss (1967) were the first to describe the idea of **grounded theory** and its uses in social research. In the decades following their collaboration, Strauss pursued a more qualitative vision for grounded theory, while Glaser advocated a more quantitative path. The methodology has gained greatest attention among qualitative researchers interested in providing greater structure to the process of data collection and theory building involved in field studies.

Rather than focusing on a specific type of data, however, grounded theory is perhaps best thought of as a term that describes the interaction between the early parts of the research process that I have discussed thus far. At first, it represents a process through which data are observed, described, categorized, and is used, ultimately, to develop a rough sketch of a causal theory. However, as theory develops further, a better theoretical understanding guides the search for and classification of additional data. This two-way street, through which data guide theoretical development while theory guides further observation, is depicted by the two-way arrow in the steps of the research model depicted in Figure 1.1. For grounded theorists, theory building approaches completion when research becomes "saturated," or when "additional analysis no longer contributes to discovering anything new about a category" (Strauss, 1987, p. 21).

An example of grounded theory can be found in McLachlan and Justice's (2009, p. 28) study of the experiences of international students. In the study, the authors interview and code the responses of international students about their experiences in the United States and then, "as codes and themes were identified, the research team compared and contrasted new data to data collected previously and relationships between categories provided the grounding for building theory." The authors identify six themes associated with "transition shock" and go on to explain descriptively and interpretively how students have coped with their new experiences.

I have brought up the concept of grounded theory because it emphasizes the fact that the steps described in this chapter need not proceed in a linear fashion. Grounded theory, above all, focuses on the cyclical nature of research when theory is built "inductively." In Chapter 4, I will further examine the nature of inductively derived theory and how the methodology underlying it differs from deductively derived theory. I will also explore other types of issues that affect the nature of causal theories and the research questions they seek to explain.

Conclusion

In this chapter, I discussed the earliest steps of knowledge accumulation in the research process. First, I divided the concept of "observation" into three large categories: (1) first-person observation, (2) "opinion-seeking" research, and (3) "media"-ted data collection, which involves collecting data from some intermediary source. I then subdivided each category into a qualitative and quantitative subcategory and discussed different approaches to in-depth data collection.

I also looked at how description entails the basic organization of raw data into a coherent framework. Furthermore, I differentiated descriptive research, which deals with basic facts involving who, what, where, and when of an event, from causal research that seeks to understand why and how things happen and is the subject of Chapter 4.

During much of the final part of the chapter, I discussed issues involved in the classification of descriptive information. Classification of data helps bring out the natural grouping and connections between like phenomena and aids further causal research by establishing a framework through which cause-and-effect relationships can be analyzed. The conceptualization of "latent" variables also provides the basis for "operationalization" processes that I will discuss in Chapter 4.

As a final point, I should emphasize that not all research projects involve the type of basic research that I discussed in this chapter. Different research projects begin at different places in the research process depending on the goals of a researcher and the amount of preexisting information that exists about a subject. However, even when a project is based on earlier theories or assumptions, the research that originally went into those theories and assumptions began with efforts of earlier researchers to seek out, understand, and organize information.

DISCUSSION QUESTIONS

2.1 Come up with a social situation in which participant observation could be used to collect data. What is the goal of the project? Are there ethical implications involved in your participation?

2.2 Come up with a list of three to four intangible concepts/constructs that a social scientist might want to better understand. Pick one and make your own conceptual map. Are the bottom subconcepts mutually exclusive and exhaustive without being redundant?

2.3 Imagine that a group of students were asked to self-assess their personality traits on a numerical scale. The correlations between their responses are reported on the following correlation matrix.

	Happy	Intelligent	Lazy	Honest
Happy	x			
Intelligent	.45	x		
Lazy	−.15	−.55	x	
Honest	.33	.02	−.65	x

Which of the variables are most closely correlated with one another?

Which variables are weakly correlated with one another?

What do the signs indicate about the relationships?

2.4 In the days leading up to the 2012 U.S. presidential election, most prominent polls predicted reelection for President Obama. However, several pollsters predicted a victory for challenger Mitt Romney, arguing that many of the other polling models were built on faulty assumptions. What types of assumptions must pollsters make when relying on stratified sampling to make electoral predictions, and how can these assumptions affect their predictions?

Appendix to Chapter 2

Literature Reviews

Although the primary focus of this book is on broader methodological concepts, the topic of literature review is such an important nuts-and-bolts practical matter that it merits a bit of extended discussion. While the ultimate goal of research lies with discovering new things, uncovering new data, and arriving at novel understandings of phenomena, an essential part of learning new things is understanding what has already been done. Literature review helps a researcher understand what has been studied and what yet needs to be learned. It also helps a researcher better understand how a subject has been studied and might lead a researcher to come up with his or her alternate approach to understanding a subject.

Discussing literature review involves discussing two separate, but interrelated, topics. First, there is the process of finding and paging through dozens, if not more, sources that are related to a researcher's question of interest. This is the process of reviewing related literature. Second, there is the question of how to "write up" and convey to an audience the essential features of that search and how a researcher's project and eventual findings fit into a broader theoretical framework.

The Process of Reviewing Literature

There are no real rules or conventions for delving into the literature as a researcher attempts to familiarize himself or herself with a topic. At the early stages of a project, almost any type of source can provide useful ideas for better formulating and narrowing down a research question. During these earliest, "exploratory" phases of literature review, researchers tend to privilege the breadth of sources over an in-depth examination of particular sources. Loseke (2013) describes the importance of skimming scholarly works, suggesting that one should

> start with the abstracts. Abstracts are short, so you can read them carefully. Look for the research question, the data generation techniques, the sample, and the major findings. Some articles that have interesting titles will turn out to be of little or no use to you. If that is the case, then go on to the next article. Only if there seems to be something interesting should you continue to read the actual article. (p. 60)

Beyond abstracts, the initial skimming process will also entail browsing through the introductions and conclusions of scholarly works as well as the works cited/reference pages of these materials. The last point about the reference pages at the end of books and articles is particularly useful as these will help direct the researcher to some of the most relevant sources, and the reference sections in the new sources will help the researcher locate even more sources and so on.

A comprehensive literature review necessarily entails a high "dross rate." *Dross* is a term used in qualitative research to describe extraneous information that is initially gathered but eventually discarded. At the beginning of research, it is often useful to collect as many sources as possible and then later sift through and prioritize the available information, disregarding what lacks relevance.

As the relevance of different sources becomes clearer to a researcher, the process of actually reading books and articles becomes more in-depth. It is important to prioritize the relevance of different materials as best as possible and concentrate more on the areas most central to the research question that is being developed. Many a would-be researcher has become too bogged down in the early stages of reviewing literature by spending too much time reading sources of limited relevance. An old saying during my years of graduate study was that the best way to avoid writing one's dissertation was to read another book! Reviewing other people's works is important, but doing so should supplement, not subtract from or substitute for, the original research that lies ahead.

Writing a Literature Review

The goals of a written literature review are to convey the context of a researcher's project in relationship to other similar studies, to communicate what research has already been conducted, and to inform the reader what a researcher plans to do (or has already done) differently. A literature review is an organized compilation of *secondary sources* that describe the findings and conclusions of others researchers. It is different from simple "background information" in that it focuses on the interpretations and findings of other scholars.

There is no one-size-fits-all approach to writing literature reviews. Different research fields often have different conventions and expectations about the focus, format, and extensiveness of such reviews. Even within the same field, literature reviews may appear as a self-contained section, be divided into several sections, be integrated into an introductory section or chapter, or appear diffused and "piecemeal" throughout a work.

There are a few commonalities, however, that characterize most discussions of other scholarly works. They are usually organized by theoretical "theme," beginning with a brief discussion of studies that are more tangentially related to a researcher's work and then progressing to a more in-depth discussion of works that are more closely related. The figure included in this appendix offers a simple pictorial representation of the "inverted triangle" that characterizes the structure of most literature reviews. The broad top of the triangle represents the broader themes reflected in the early parts of a literature review, with the narrowing of the sides to a point representing the movement toward the researcher's specific subject matter.

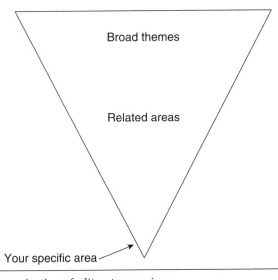

General organization of a literature review

What is generally thought of as an incorrect manner of structuring literature reviews is referred to by Johnson and Reynolds (2008) as the "boxcar method" (p. 201). The boxcar method is characterized by repeated passive summarization of different sources. Instead of paragraphs that are organized thematically, a writer of a boxcar-style literature review introduces paragraphs with sentences like "in his book, so and so says. . ." and then proceeds to simply summarize each work. While devoting an entire paragraph to discussing a specific source or author might be appropriate toward the end of a literature review, the main goal is to group several authors' arguments and findings together in similarly themed paragraphs.

It is important not to overcomplicate the idea of writing a literature review. Whether organizing one thematically or in some other sensible fashion—such as chronologically—the main point is to present a pared-down discussion of the process of reviewing literature that a researcher conducts at the outset of (and often throughout) a project, while also providing an organized framework for understanding other scholars' earlier work.

3

Causal Theory

Overview

This chapter focuses on developing causal theory, a process that lies at the heart of most research projects. The discussion examines broad traditions in theory building across a variety of disciplines. It explores the differences in deriving theory inductively, through processes of observation, description, and classification, as well as how one can arrive at theory deductively based on assumptions that are logical and/or mathematical in nature.

The chapter also examines the differences and connections between causal theories that are based on **qualitative research**, which analyzes a small number of things in greater detail, and **quantitative research**, which attempts to understand larger-scale trends. This discussion of the "qualitative–quantitative" spectrum discusses the advantages and disadvantages of both types of research while illustrating the types of questions that each research tradition tends to address.

There is also a discussion of levels of analysis that connects macro-, mid-, and microlevel analyses with the concepts of qualitative, quantitative, deductive, and inductive reasoning. The chapter provides detailed examples of major traditions that illustrate each of these approaches, introducing terms such as **phenomenalism**, **structuralism**, and **behavioralism**.

Last, the final discussion of the chapter suggests how researchers think about the process of building theories either inductively or deductively. After a brief discussion of deductive reasoning, the chapter provides step-by-step suggestions for students and scholars thinking about how to build the strongest inductive arguments possible.

Introduction

It is one thing to know what happened, it is another thing to know why and how something happened. This chapter is about the leap researchers take when they move from the description of events to arguments about why those events happen. The process of causal theorizing is fraught with peril because another layer of interpretation is added on top of the interpretation that went into collecting, analyzing, and organizing raw data. As such, there rarely exists an "unassailable" causal theory that is impervious to questioning, refinement, and even negation after additional information is uncovered or new understandings developed.

One obstacle to understanding causality is that it can rarely be observed. Causality tends to be invisible. For instance, if I witness someone being hit by a car, I can say what happened, but I cannot necessarily say why. Even if I uncover more information, for instance, that the driver was drunk or the pedestrian was jaywalking, how can I be sure that one, the other, or both factors contributed to the accident?

Another obstacle to understanding causality is that many things happen probabilistically rather than deterministically. While I can surely make a case that drunk driving is more likely to cause someone to strike a pedestrian, the majority of drunk drivers arrive home without incident on a given night (please don't try this) and most jaywalkers cross the road in one piece. Causal trends are harder to come to terms with than causal absolutes. Unless a researcher is investigating the type of deterministic event that always happens the same way, arguments about causality can be difficult to make.

While there is no perfect way to build causal arguments, some approaches are better than others. I investigate, in this chapter, the ways that researchers attempt to make sense of causality and how they create the best arguments possible about why and how things happen. I discuss broad approaches to theory building and provide examples from a variety of fields that reflect different ways of approaching different types of research questions.

What Is Causal Theory?

As researchers, our ultimate goal is usually to understand, to the best of our abilities, how and why things happen. While many excellent projects focus on questions concerning where and when something occurs and what or who was responsible for the occurrence, the final piece of the puzzle addresses how something occurs.

The term *theory*, like many other terms used when discussing research, can mean different things to different people. Theory suggests something abstract—something that is the opposite of "empirical." The abstract nature of theory arises from the very goals of theory building, namely, to explain causal relationships that cannot be witnessed in person.

Theory also involves uncertainty. For some, the phrase "it's just a theory" implies that the uncertainty inherent in theory is its defining characteristic. The uncertain nature of theory arises from the fact that efforts to develop causal theories rely heavily on assumptions or inferences about unobservable phenomena. As a matter of fact, no theory can be proven with 100% certainty. Theories, like court cases, vary in strength from the merely plausible to those that are widely accepted as beyond a reasonable doubt. The strength of a theory arises from the evidence used to support the theory, how well the theory seems to explain observable reality, as well as, it must be admitted, the opinion of those evaluating the theory.

Theories are more complex than simple hypotheses or factual descriptions. Theories range in ambition from small-scale causal explanations to entire bodies of knowledge with a range of subtheories and interrelated propositions. However, even though theory is sometimes described as a "body of knowledge," causality, not complexity, is its defining feature. As a matter of fact, it is universally accepted that the principle of **parsimony**,[1] the ability to "explain the most with the least" (without compromising explanatory power) is a desirable feature of a good theory. That being said, a theory that does explain more is better than one that explains less, all other things being equal.

In summary, a theory can be thought as a proposition or set of propositions that (a) explains causal relationships; (b) is abstract, in the sense that the causal relationships are inferred rather than observed directly; (c) has a degree of uncertainty, even if very well supported; and (d) may range in ambition and complexity.

The scope and nature of theories vary greatly depending on the goals of researchers and the research questions that are being pursued. The following pages detail a variety of different approaches to theory building. Some theories are built inductively, others deductively. Some theories attempt to explain particular circumstances, others general trends, and,

---

1. One of the fancier ways of describing parsimony is to invoke the principle of "Ockam's (or Occam's) Razor." The term is associated with the medieval monk, William of Ockam, whose approach to philosophy was seen as one in which extraneous argument had been "shaved away" in the search for simpler truths.

yet others, universal causality. I also discuss some examples of theoretical traditions in the social sciences to illustrate how different research agendas inform different types of theoretical thinking. Finally, I discuss how a researcher goes about building his or her own theory.

Deriving Theories Inductively and Deductively

Although there is an element of inspiration and creativity involved in developing new theories, causal explanations do not simply pop out of thin air into a researcher's head. They are built on preexisting knowledge. How preexisting knowledge is arranged and employed to arrive at a plausible theory depends on whether a research problem is tackled through *inductive* or *deductive* reasoning (see Figure 3.1).

Inductive reasoning is generally defined as reasoning from the "specific to the general" while **deductive reasoning** is defined as reasoning from "general to the specific." These definitions are somewhat problematic, however. In the case of inductive reasoning, a researcher might infer a specific, rather than a general, cause to a particular observation. For instance, a doctor might observe a patient and come to inductively believe that a specific illness is causing that patient distress. Similarly troublesome for traditional definitions, deductive reasoning might arrive at a general theory from a general set of assumptions. Einstein's $E = mc^2$ is a

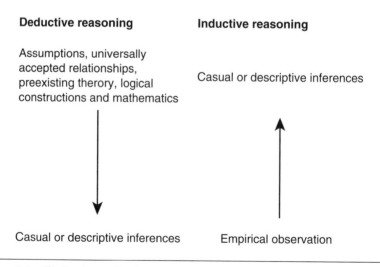

Figure 3.1:   Deductive and inductive reasoning

universal theory deduced from equally universal propositions.

It is best to simply think of deductive and inductive reasoning in terms of how each reasoning process begins. Is a researcher using observation or unobserved assumptions/theories as the starting point of the reasoning process? If the process begins with observation, then the process can be described as inductive; if the process begins with a preexisting theory or set of assumptions, then it is deductive.

To make things more complex, theory building often employs both types of reasoning. The assumptions of a deductive theory were, presumably, inductively derived at some point. With inductive theory building, the search for data not only informs causal theory, but as causal theory is developed, it deductively informs the process of further data collection. Furthermore, even when a theory is inductively derived, it may represent the jumping-off point for the deduction of hypotheses and the empirical assessment of its viability. In the following discussion, I describe inductive and deductive theory building in as simple terms as possible. However, in reality, the research process often does not necessarily proceed straight from point A to point B, either inductively or deductively, in such a direct manner.

Inductive Reasoning

Inductive reasoning is much more intuitive for most people than deductive reasoning. This is because we frequently employ inductive reasoning in our everyday lives. Inductive reasoning entails drawing descriptive or causal conclusions from a limited set of observations. For instance, when I notice that raccoons disappear from my yard during the winter, I might theorize that raccoons hibernate in the winter. If I buy a car that promptly breaks down, I might conclude that the company that built it sells inferior-quality cars.

One of the most famous employers of inductive reasoning was the fictional detective Sherlock Holmes. Even though the character was famous for using the phrase "I deduce," in reality, Holmes would come up with his (factual-descriptive) theories about the perpetrators of crime based on evidence he observed in his environment. The process of deriving conclusions from observations is classic inductive reasoning.

Since inductive reasoning, by definition, relies on the observation and description of a particular event or process, the entire first part of the research model found in Figure 1.1 as well as the material discussed in Chapter 2 reflect inductive approaches to the construction of theory (Figure 3.2 shows a simplified version of Figure 1.1 that reflects inductive and deductive directionality). Observation and description of observed

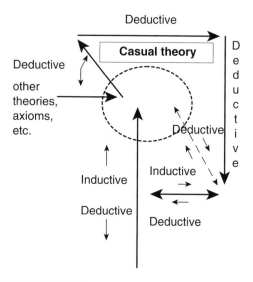

Figure 3.2:   Deductive and inductive reasoning in the research model (Figure 1.1)

data are primarily inductive processes. Archaeologists may use inductive reasoning to theorize about the way of life of earlier civilizations based on artifacts they find, and psychologists may inductively infer childhood trauma from present-day mental disorders in particular patients.

Using observational data to develop theories of causality, however, presents problems. Since causality may only be inferred rather than directly observed, causality is initially derived from the judgment of the observer and reinforced by circumstantial evidence that may suggest alternate explanations. If, for instance, a researcher inductively arrives at the conclusion that students with poor test scores simply are not working hard enough, but cannot actually observe their work habits in their home, he or she might easily be drawing the wrong conclusion. Perhaps the students have learning disabilities but work hard. Or maybe they work hard, but their secondary schools prepared them poorly for college. Or maybe testing procedures are unrepresentative of student effort. Maybe it is a combination of different things. How do we proceed to draw causal conclusions when there are so many legitimate explanations?

When reasoning inductively, it is important to establish the plausibility of a theory by systematically eliminating alternate explanations—a process I describe later in this chapter. Even when the causality posited through inductive reasoning seems to be the "most plausible" explanation, inductive arguments leave a lot of room for error. There is always the chance that our set of samples is not representative of the general population or that any patterns we observe, we do so through random chance. For example, we might observe a coin being flipped that ends up heads 10 times, 100 times, or 1,000 times in a row through sheer chance without any trick being played on us. Like any other inductive theory, we can infer that a coin ending up heads 1,000 times in a row is probably double sided. However, it might also be the case that we were very (un)lucky, the coin is legitimate, and that the next time it will come up heads.

Ultimately, an inductive theory is an argument based on the weight of the evidence available to a researcher. The argument might be a strong one, but it can never be "airtight." Inductive reasoning, however, approaches theory in a much different manner than deductive reasoning, which I describe next.

Deductive Reasoning

Deductive theory building is most commonly found in the natural sciences, economics, and "formal" social science theories of human behavior. In the natural sciences, deductive theory is more common in "theoretical" fields, such as particle physics, where phenomena are often not directly observable. Einstein's mathematically complex theories of relativity were purely deductive, and its elements were only *subsequently* subject to empirical observation and analysis. Economic models are built around assumptions concerning human preferences and how these preferences would be expected to result in particular behaviors. Macrostructural theories, like Marxism, are not necessarily constructed around formal mathematics but make similar deductions about how, given a certain set of circumstances, human beings (or larger units of analysis like classes or countries) would express regular patterns of interaction.

Deductive theories draw on preexisting knowledge to build new theories. Formal logic is employed to argue cause and effect rather than the more informal "pattern recognition" of empirical data that characterizes inductive reasoning. Deductive theory building often draws on other, better established, theories. Theoreticians deduce further consequences and seek to improve or challenge the premises on which earlier theories are built.

For example, the Austrian priest Gregor Mendel inductively derived from his studies of pea plants the idea that certain traits follow hereditary patterns. However, his theories later served as the source of subsequent

20th-century deductions by later geneticists who used his research on dominant and recessive genes as the starting point for their own work.

Thus, unlike inductively derived theories, purely deductively derived theories never originate from scratch. More often, they represent an attempt to build on, and formalize, preexisting information and theories. By utilizing the universal rules of logic and other formal mathematics, deductively derived theories also usually tend to be "macro" in their implications.

The correctness of the conclusions of deductive theory is, in principle, based on the correctness of the premises on which the theory is built. Subsequently inferred relationships are "airtight" if the deductive argument is based on sound logic (which is often mathematical in nature). This approach differs significantly from inductive reasoning, which, since it is based on observer inference, requires a strong "weight-of-the-evidence" argument to be made in favor of the causal relationships posited.

One of the problems with deductive reasoning, however, is that the world, and particularly human behavior, often does not function with the clockwork precision that the assumptions of deductive theory demand. While inductive theories are vulnerable to critique in terms of the interpretation of empirical evidence, deductive theories are most vulnerable when they rest on questionable assumptions. In the mathematically precise world of the natural sciences, this is less of a problem. In the social sciences, however, assumptions about social interactions are always open to question.

On the other hand, formal deduction is useful for the clarity it brings to theory building. Correct or not, the underlying assumptions are clearly expressed, and interrelationships are clearly laid out in a parsimonious way that avoids many of the potential contradictions and ad hoc reasoning that a less rigorously derived theory might contain. Later in this chapter, I describe in greater detail some of the forms that deductive theory building may take.

Next, I discuss how different theories vary in the scope and depth of their causal propositions depending on the nature of different research projects. The most basic and well-known divide, especially in the social sciences, is between so-called qualitative and quantitative research.

Qualitative and Quantitative Theory and Research

Research questions and subsequent research agendas vary greatly in the scope of the subject matter studied. Questions of causality might address everything from why one thing happens to why everything happens. In the early 20th century, the German philosopher Wilhelm Windelband suggested dividing causal theory into two types: (1) **idiographic**, which is Latin for "particularistic," and (2) **nomothetic**, or "proposition of the law."

Which type of causal theory a project investigates depends on the nature of the subject matter. Idiographic theory, or **microlevel theory**, examines the behavior and nature of specific people, groups, or events. Nomothetic theory takes a more top-down approach to theory and attempts to uncover trends from available data in order to predict universal regularities.

In practice, however, a whole range of research questions exists between the extreme poles represented by idiographic contextualism and nomothetic universalism. Most research involves investigating groups of subjects that are neither singular nor all inclusive. *Qualitative* research reflects a more idiographically oriented approach that examines smaller numbers of things or people (cases) in greater detail, while *quantitative* research sacrifices this detail for inclusiveness and examines a large number of cases.

There is no magical dividing line between the qualitative and quantitative work. Instead, a spectrum or continuum, rather than a dichotomy, exists with many projects best characterized as more qualitative or more quantitative rather than purely idiographic or nomethetic. Nevertheless, some fields clearly favor one type of approach over the other. Research that is conducted in the humanities is almost exclusively qualitative and focuses on human experiences and perceptions. Research conducted in the natural sciences is almost exclusively quantitative and focuses on patterns of behavior of organisms and objects from tiny to enormous scales. Social scientists, on the other hand, occupy the large middle ground, with different traditions focusing on anything from qualitative social interactions to large-scale social trends (see Figure 3.3).

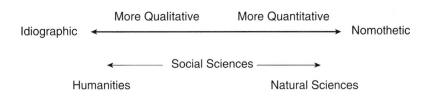

Figure 3.3:   The qualitative–quantitative spectrum

The type of research pursued, whether qualitative or quantitative, is first and foremost determined by the type of research question that is under investigation. As I describe in the next section, each type of research has its advantages and disadvantages in building and assessing convincing causal theory. These trade-offs are inherent in the subject matter under investigation, however, not as a consequence of the superiority of one approach to another.

Qualitative Theory and Research

Qualitative research is most associated with the humanities and certain types of social science. The subject-centered nature of qualitative research lends itself to questions that are specific to certain settings, time periods, and people. Thus, a sociologist examining racial attitudes by interviewing members of a particular country club would be engaged in qualitative research in contrast to survey research examining racial attitudes among golfers in general. Similarly, an anthropologist examining why Kalahari tribespeople have turned increasingly toward an agrarian way of life would be engaged in qualitative theorizing, so too would a psychologist engaged in the study of a particular emotionally troubled patient.

Qualitative research attempts to understand relationships underlying a particular single case or small number of particular events, which is why **case study research** is by nature more qualitative. Case studies are, in fact, the backbone of qualitative research used to inductively understand both what happened and why things happened. I will discuss further in Chapter 6 how case studies can be used both inductively and deductively (or both), depending on the nature of a study.

Qualitative research is particularly useful for understanding human perceptions and motivations in a way that top-down quantitative research cannot. A commonly used phrase among some qualitative researchers is the term **Verstehen**, which indicates a deep and contextual understanding of the motivations and perceptions of those being studied. Put more plainly, perceptual "understanding," rather than objectivity, is the core concept of much qualitative research. Qualitative scholarship usually depends on focusing on a small number of people or events while forgoing the ability to investigate more general trends.

Not all qualitative research focuses on subjective perceptions, however. The defining feature of qualitative research is not its specific subject matter, **ontological** underpinning, or approach (and there are many, many specific qualitative methods!), but rather that qualitative researchers focus on a smaller number of cases than quantitative researchers. Sometimes, this means perceptual research, other times, it simply means adopting a more traditional *positivist* investigation of a specific case or small number of cases. **Comparative methodologies**, for example, investigate a small number of cases and suggest tentative theories about causal relationships without usually delving too deeply in perceptual issues. The differing goals and understandings of qualitative-interpretivist approaches compared with qualitative-positivist approaches is often as significant as the differences in qualitatively versus quantitatively oriented research.

Whatever the specific approach, all types of qualitative research share a similar limitation. What qualitative research can achieve in terms of the depth of knowledge obtained about a particular subject in a particular context is not always readily applied to a different situation and setting. Qualitative knowledge is good at understanding a particular thing but not particularly well suited for understanding the way of things. To better understand how things tend to behave, in general, we must look to quantitative theory and research.

Quantitative Theory and Research

While qualitative-oriented theory focuses on particular subjects and contexts, quantitative-oriented theory examines larger numbers of cases in an attempt to uncover general trends. Often quantitative research is associated with words such as "statistics" and "regression analysis." Such tools are often used to help understand trends in data when large numbers of cases are involved. Data that are collected quantitatively differ from that collected qualitatively because they are measured and enumerated from the outset. Data that are analyzed quantitatively make use of descriptive (Chapter 2) and inferential (Chapter 5) statistical methods. Research that is thought of in general as "quantitative research" seeks to understand broad trends involving the characteristics or cause-and-effect relationships inherent among many different subjects.

Quantitative research differs from qualitative research in its goals, advantages, and shortcomings. More so than qualitative theory, quantitative theory yields conclusions that can more convincingly predict the behavior of subjects beyond the area of immediate study. For instance, medical scientists might study the effect of zinc supplements on colds in a particular group and then be able to predict that other people will have similar reactions. Such generalizations must be approached much more tentatively in qualitative research.

If quantitative research is more widely applicable, why not approach every qualitative problem by studying as many cases as possible? Simply put, not every research question has larger ramifications outside of itself. Although the search for "law-like generalizations" can be fruitful, some situations are unique with their own set of factors existing in a particular context. Although the question of why political leaders are assassinated is interesting, a research question specifically addressing President Lincoln's assassination would entail an examination of a unique circumstance with unique actors and motivations.

When it comes to developing sophisticated causal theories, qualitative approaches tend to have an advantage over "bird's-eye" quantitative analysis. Qualitative research focuses on causal mechanisms in a more nuanced and complex manner than is often possible when approaching research quantitatively. Thus, qualitative theory building tends to be more sophisticated and grounded than theory developed by researchers who simply draw intuitive inferences from patterns of numerical data.

On the other hand, quantitative approaches are better at analyzing whether or not a theory is likely to be true or not. In other words, they are more verifiable. The more cases a researcher has at his or her disposal, the more information he or she has to judge whether one thing really influences another in the manner suggested by a particular causal theory. In some cases, qualitative theories cannot be empirically verified at all. In other words, they often represent unfalsifiable arguments. Quantitative research, on the other hand, often reveals patterns within data without fully or convincingly investigating the causal connections inherent therein.

In the end, the important thing for a researcher to understand when approaching a problem is what the goal of his or her research is. If the goal is "thick description" or an attempt to infer a detailed picture of causal mechanisms at work, then qualitative research will likely be the correct approach. If the goal of a researcher is to understand general trends and verify whether such trends exist, then quantitative methods are preferable. As Newman and Benz (1998) write,

> When faced with the question, "Which is better?" we would refuse to answer; indeed we would be *unable* to answer, given the choices presented. There is no such answer. The better paradigm (qualitative or quantitative) is the one that serves to answer the specific research question. (p. 111)

Mixed Methods

Some researchers tackle research questions by using a combination of qualitative and quantitative methods. Although others, particularly those eschewing a positivist worldview, have rejected using such a "mixed-method" approach (this assertion is known simply as the "incompatibility thesis"), it is common practice to combine methodologies to some degree. Other methodologists such as Teddlie and Tashakkori (2003), in a 700-page edited "handbook" on the subject, argue that mixed methods represents a distinct tradition unto itself and that their usage is set to become "the dominant methodological tools in the social and behavioral sciences in the 21st century" (p. 8).

Those who advocate using mixed methods see qualitative and quantitative research as fruitfully complementing one another. Mixing methods is colorfully advocated, for instance, by the well-known statistical forecaster Nate Silver (2012) who discusses how scouting and statistical analysis complement each other in recruiting baseball players:

> If Prospect A is hitting .300 with twenty home runs and works at a soup kitchen during his off days, and Prospect B is hitting .300 with twenty home runs but hits up night clubs and snorts coke during his free time, there is probably no way to *quantify* this distinction. But you'd sure as hell want to take it into account. (p. 100)

There are two main ways that more qualitatively oriented research might be combined with more quantitatively oriented research. The first way is by using both methodologies at the same stages of the research process—particularly in respect to information gathering and analysis associated with inductive theory building. Methodologically speaking, the term triangulation implies investigating a question from different angles in an attempt to realize the benefits of each approach. For example, Weyers, Strydom, and Huisamen (2011) conducted a study on the effects of a "self-management" training program for the social work branch of the South African Police Service that combined a quantitative analysis of attitudinal changes with qualitative analysis of how participants felt about the program and its effect on their lives. Similarly, Goerres and Prinzen (2012) examine German attitudes toward the welfare state through a combination of interviewing and statistical analysis of questionnaires.

Another way of mixing qualitative and quantitative research is by using different methods at different stages of the research process rather than concurrently. For instance, the strength of case study research lies in its ability to help a researcher understand causal mechanisms in detail. Such case study research might be used to inductively derive a theory of causality whose elements could later be tested through quantitative data collection and analysis. A recent example of this type of project was an extensive study conducted by the World Bank, which studied how health care expansion was implemented in 22 countries, each of which was studied using country-specific case studies (which themselves combined qualitative and quantitative techniques). Following those studies, statistical analysis was used to better understand health care reform trends across all of the countries studied (Giedion, Alfonso, & Diaz, 2013).

While sometimes quantitative analysis might follow qualitative theory building, other times, the reverse is true. Sometimes a qualitative analysis follows a quantitative analysis to better understand the findings of the quantitative work and how it addresses the research question being addressed. This use of case studies in deconstructing earlier quantitative efforts is part of the discussion in Chapter 6, which addresses how bringing theory into the "real world" helps researchers learn how previously derived theories and findings translate into practical knowledge.

Theoretical Levels of Analysis

Research and theoretical development may occur at different levels of analysis that reflect different assumptions about who or what causes something to happen. Sometimes things happen because of decisions people make, and sometimes things happen because larger societal, political, and economic forces are at work. Causal theory may be divided into *micro-*, *macro-*, and *midlevel approaches*.[2] Microlevel studies study how the perceptions, understandings, motivations, and actions of individuals and small groups influence outcomes. On the other side of the spectrum, macrolevel or "grand" studies see causality as systemic and originating from broad, often impersonal structures and forces. Midlevel theorists occupy a broad middle ground and are usually grounded in positivist, inductive traditions that seek to analyze statistical trends associated with a particular phenomenon.

---

2. Many scholars, on the other hand, simply differentiate between micro- and macrolevels. Different fields also may label these levels of analysis in different ways. The differences I draw between micro-, macro-, and midlevel analysis, like many subjects in methodology, is inherently subjective to a certain degree.

Imagine that a researcher wanted to approach the question of why certain neighborhoods have more crime than others. A macrolevel theorist might seek to understand why the opportunities for people in a particular neighborhood were more limited than those in a different neighborhood. In this case, the primary source of causality under investigation might involve culture, economics, or other societal influences.

A microlevel theorist would approach the questions differently. Some might conduct interviews to better understand the outlook of people in the neighborhood. Others might seek to weigh the choices and incentives that someone might face when choosing whether or not to seek an education or a life of crime. In these cases, the individual is the primary causal actor.

A midlevel theorist would examine data on different neighbors and attempt to determine what variables most account for poverty. Unlike macrolevel theorists, midlevel theorists tend to collect information and formulate theories inductively. Most likely, quantitative data would be collected from either city records or some other source. A midlevel theorist would start off with a theory suggesting which factors caused poverty, seek to eliminate less plausible explanations, and then statistically assess those that remained.

Main Traditions in Theory Building in the Social Sciences

In this section, I illustrate the concepts of induction and deduction as well as different levels of theoretical analysis by discussing major research traditions in the social sciences. The first subsection focuses on "interpretivist" traditions that rely on inductive research to create "thickly" descriptive accounts of events and qualitative theories. A subset of microlevel theory, interpretivist research is often considered the most qualitative of all research due to its focus on human interactions, motivations, and perceptions. The second and third subsections focus on theories that rely on deductive reasoning, including structuralist theories that suggest how large "macrolevel" forces in society influence behavior and rational choice theories, which seek to explain how individual choices are made. The last section takes a deeper look at "midlevel"-type research, which is associated with the terms **positivism**, **realism**, and even *the scientific method*.

The Interpretivist Tradition: Microlevel Induction

The approach to research taken by interpretivists varies significantly from that taken by the more empirical-minded scholars. This is a product of different ontological assumptions—that is to say assumptions about the nature of reality itself. More empirical-minded traditions tend to view the social and natural worlds as made up of measurable and ultimately, given the right resources, verifiable interactions and processes. The purists within the interpretivist tradition, on the other hand, hold that "measurement of social life is not possible or . . . that the things that can be measured are meaningless or unimportant" (Abbott, 2004, p. 43).

The term *interpretivist* encompasses numerous traditions in qualitative research that focus on firsthand observation and interviewing as the primary mode of data collection. Such research focuses on a single case or small number of cases in particular contexts and eschews the idea that legitimate research needs to be verified through quantitative-based analysis. Many interpretivists would also consider themselves *constructivists*—that is to say that they believe that social meaning is an interactive learning process that is "constructed" through the process of social interaction.

Although the **interpretivist approaches** differ somewhat from one another in their underlying assumptions, a common thread tying them together is the personal involvement of the researcher with his or her subject matter. Rather than maintaining an objective distance from the subject at hand, interpretivists take a much more hands-on approach by actively placing themselves within the social processes that are being researched. The goal of such research is not the uncovering of trends or "law-like generalizations" but, rather, the furtherance of *Verstehen*, or deep interpretative understanding. Fields as diverse as feminism, nursing studies, literary analysis, cultural anthropology, and historical "postmodernism" rely heavily on these types of approaches and the understandings that underlie them.

Two of the most important terms in interpretivist research are *phenomenalism* and **ethnography**. Phenomenological studies examine the "meaning of several people's lived experiences around a specific issue or phenomenon," and ethnographic studies seek "the description and interpretation of a cultural or social group or system" (Cresswell, 1998, p. 58). Phenomenalism tends to be more of a guiding principle or ontological understanding in a variety of different types of research endeavors, while ethnography describes a more specific research agenda. Both words are central, however, to the activities of much interpretativist research as well as how interprevatist researchers go about viewing the world.

Phenomenalism

The term *phenomenon*, as it was originally utilized by Immanuel Kant (and many who followed), refers to the perceptual awareness of things around us. It suggests that we cannot remove ourselves from our own senses and directly witness "things as they are." In contrast to positivist traditions, this implies a permanent distancing of facts from observable data. For the *phenomenalist* researcher, then, the most interesting realm of discovery lies not in chasing down unknowable facts but, rather, in attempting to understand the world through the varied ways individuals perceive reality. Phenomenologists "seek to *sense* reality and describe it in words, rather than numbers—words that reflect consciousness and perception" (Bernard, 2000, p. 20).

The most direct way of gaining a better understanding of individuals' perceptions is to talk to them. Thus, interviewing subjects is the foremost method involved in this research tradition. In contrast to interviews that might be conducted for survey purposes or other more structured endeavors, phenomenalist research consciously adopts interviewing techniques that are largely unstructured with the goal of understanding "the complex behavior of members of society without imposing any a priori categorization that may limit the field of inquiry." (Fontana & Frey, 1994, p. 366).

Another guiding principle of this type of research involves the concept of "reflexivity." Reflexivity suggests that the researcher, in learning about a subject's perceptions, is also learning about themselves in the process. Indeed, a cornerstone principle of this type of research is that a researcher cannot, and should not, divorce himself or herself from the subject being interviewed. The subject also becomes part of a "democratic relationship" (Glicken, 2003, p. 31) that relies on his or her participation in guiding the direction of the endeavor.

The objective of such research is usually to create a narrative "story" that involves "thick," detailed description. The description focuses on the situational outlooks and concerns of the participants. Qualitative "theorizing" becomes part of the endeavor when descriptive elements are interpreted as causal factors involved in a social event or events. For instance, an understanding and description of African American perceptions toward the Los Angeles Police Department in the early 1990s might provide important clues to the outbreak of rioting in the city in 1992. In such a case, perceptions of members of the African American community are not only important in their own right but also serve as the basis for causal inquiry into a historical event.

Ethnography

Ethnography incorporates principles of phenomenalism in the qualitative study of group interactions and culture within a given setting. The focus is usually not on hard data or rigorous theory building but rather on learning new information about human relationships. Sociologists and anthropologists, in particular, are associated with this type of research.

In an ethnographic study, researchers investigate cultural processes and norms of social groups within particular settings. Often these social groups are "ethnic" groups, but in other cases, they might also be members of a particular location, class, or occupation. While ethnography might employ techniques such as interviewing or document or visual media research, participant observation is the method with which ethnography is most associated.

When a researcher actively interacts with the members of a community being studied, he or she is engaged in participant observation. How much the researcher is a participant and how much he or she is an observer depends on the nature of the project. Either way, information is gathered "in the field" (as opposed to through research of documents or other situationally removed methods). Ethnographic research often takes place over relatively long periods of time, often a year or more.

One example of a recent long-term ethnographic study involved a 16-month examination of patients, nurses, and doctors in a coronary care unit. The study by Wolf, Ekman, and Dellenborg (2012) examines how the professionals perceived one another, how they perceived their own roles, and how each group spent their time. The study particularly focuses on "feelings"—a term the authors use no less than 17 times in their article! Although other authors might incorporate some quantitative aspects, such as response coding, into their research, their study draws primarily from intepretivist traditions that focus on description and perception.

The value of interpretative studies, in general, lies in their attempts to address questions that are difficult or impossible to evaluate empirically. The realm of human perception and symbolic understanding might be ascertained in some part through certain scientific tools such as brain scans, but it is unlikely that any technology will ever adequately capture the sum of parts that make up human thought and socialization. Interpretivist scholars attempt to capture the human condition in writing and help others understand what it is to be like someone else by a microlevel perspective that other more sweeping approaches cannot mimic.

On the other hand, because of the intangible nature of the subject matter that is examined, there is no way to verify many of the assertions of the research. Methodological issues central to other research traditions—such as whether a group is representative of a larger whole or whether the research is replicable by others—are not considered central to the interpretivist enterprise.

Furthermore, the presentation of any idiographic theory based on inductively collected information about human perception and interaction processes entails a large degree of educated guesswork. Another researcher might draw other conclusions than those drawn by a particular interpretive researcher. Nevertheless, while true verification of causal theory might be impossible, strong interpretative research can still paint a compelling picture of the perceptions and psychological and cultural motivations that underlie and influence social life.

Rational Choice Theory: Micro- and Macrolevel Deductions

Unlike the deeply contextual and perceptual inductive research underlying interpretivist approaches, **rational choice** theorists model human behavior as a product of explicit preferences and choices. The assumption that people act "rationally" often underlies causal theories in the social sciences. In the most formal type of rational choice theory, like that often encountered in economics models, scholars use mathematical equations to analyze and derive expected outcomes in human behavior.

Theories of rational choice draw on different levels of analysis depending on who the main actors, or players, are. International relations scholars or macroeconomists, for instance, might model the expected behavior of countries as they interact with one another. A microeconomist, on the other hand, would examine how individuals (or businesses, or similar small-scale actors) make the choices they make. A well-known example of the use of rational choice theory used in **game theory** is provided in the appendix at the end of the chapter.

What then, does the "rational" in rational choice suggest about human behavior? Rational choice simply assumes that people will consistently choose, in a sort of (usually informal) cost–benefit analysis,[3] options they

---

3. Some people conflate the fact that rational choice analysis involves some degree of mathematics with the idea that decision makers make choices through the same process of rigorous calculation. Rational choice theory makes no such assumptions. All that is generally required of decision making is a clear set of preferences, such as preferring ice cream to broccoli or deciding to take a test honestly versus cheating.

prefer more over options they prefer less. Rational choice theory is generally neutral about what options are "objectively" better choices, but such theory depends on assumptions about what people will prefer (e.g., more money vs. less money).

By analyzing, in the aggregate, the choices people would be expected to make given assumptions about their information, preferences, trade-offs, and rewards, formal mathematics can lead scholars to "equilibrium" outcomes that they expect people to produce individually or collectively. Other times, the analysis is less formal, and a scholar simply uses the assumptions of rational choice to help discipline his or her arguments about the costs and benefits facing people or groups as they make decisions.

The use of rational choice deductive logic to derive theories has many critics, however. Proponents of psychologically driven views of human behavior suggest that individuals are often unable or unwilling to correctly assess and make decisions that maximize their welfare (or "utility"). Factors such as risk aversion or desires for group acceptance better explain peoples' actions and would be difficult to incorporate into a rationalist framework. In addition, options and preferences might be ill-defined, or even circular.[4]

Furthermore, rational choice scholars draw large conclusions based on small numbers of assumptions. Anyone who has taken geometry class remembers deductively deriving proofs from small numbers of given "axioms" concerning the relative lengths, widths, and angles involved in different figures. However, what would happen if one of those axioms were incorrect? The whole conclusion would be invalidated. The same applies to the assumptions that underlie formal theory in the social and natural sciences.

In geometry, we can rest assured that the length of a hypotenuse really is the square root of the sum of the squares of both legs. In the social sciences, however, the "given-ness" of axioms is not always so clear. The very question of what motivates people—power, money, social norms, prestige—involve basic assumptions that often must be made for rational choice scholars to build their theories. The question also arises whether or not analysis of a given situation can ever include all the necessary factors

---

4. Circular preferences present a problem to rational choice theorists. For example, if a subject, or "player," is assumed to prefer choice A to choice B and choice B to choice C, little problem exists. The problem of circular preferences arises when the same player also prefers choice C to choice A. At this point, the mathematical logic of rational choice breaks down and further analysis is generally impossible.

involved in human interaction. Often it is difficult to present human behavior as the product of a constricted range of choices under structured conditions and preferences—no matter how elegant the solutions to the equations or statements presented.

Some of the most well-known challenges to rational choice theory have been made by Green and Shapiro (1994). The two major problems they see with rational choice scholarship in the social sciences involves how it is derived and what it represents. In terms of its derivation, many scholars they cite have created assumptions based on a small number of cases (or one case) and then worked out formulas based on those assumptions that, in turn, explain the same cases or case. Ultimately, such "curve fitting," as they describe it, establishes little outside of itself.

Their second major problem with rational choice suggests its limited use in achieving any type of empirically verifiable theory. Interestingly, the highly mathematical-minded, rational choice theoreticians face the same criticism as the highly qualitative interpretivists when it comes to the question of verification. Unlike interpretivism, which is, by nature, not often amenable to verification, deductive theories can, however, sometimes provide empirically verifiable propositions. Thus, Green and Shapiro's concern is mainly a problem concerning how some researchers employ rational choice methodology rather than the methodology itself.

Rational choice theories do achieve, however, an explicitness in theory building that is often lacked by less formal inductive theorizing. Formal theories built on rational choice assumptions make clear what the motivations underlying human decision making are thought to be and how these motivations interact with environmental factors creating different sets of expected outcomes. What rational choice theories may lack by building on simplified assumptions must be weighed against what they achieve in the clarity and rigor of the explanations they produce.

Structuralism: Macrolevel Deduction

Macrolevel *structuralist* theories suggest that humans are heavily constrained in their choices by the institutional and social "structures" within which they live. This concept of structuralism is often one of the most difficult concepts for students to grasp, because it involves the shaping of human actions by a range of organized social realities that range from the concrete (e.g., laws) to more abstract, underlying (e.g., social understandings) forces. Unlike rational choice theory, which views outcomes as being shaped by aggregate individual preferences, structural theory suggests people will act in predictable ways that are conditioned by constraints and opportunities. In other words, structuralism assumes that top-down factors influence human behavior, while rational choice builds on actor preferences and behaviors from the bottom-up.[5]

For structuralists, opportunity and perceptual structures influence human behavior such that people can be expected to behave, more or less, predictably. The opportunities that channel behavior ultimately have a greater effect on social and political outcomes than aggregate human preferences. Thus, as Lichbach (2003) elegantly states, "Structuralists maintain that analysts should study the cage rather than the prisoner" (p. 102). At the very least, most structuralists would argue that the cage and prisoner interact with one another in ways that influence both.

Although the methodological lines and labels are blurry, many *critical theorists* adopt structuralist lines of reasoning. **Critical theory** was first developed by self-proclaimed "neo-Marxists" of the "Frankfurt School" in Germany during the 1930s. While ideas linked to critical theory evolved (and eventually became associated with Jörg Habermas, its most famous proponent) over the next decades, the main basic tenets remained the same—namely, that social researchers should seek to uncover the injustices of society at the same time they expose the biases of the scholarly mainstream that favors entrenched interests.

Critical theorists focus on macrolevel societal structures that explain social and political outcomes based on inequities in power, wealth, and social status. Marxists would tend to focus on class-based explanations for social developments. Feminists often adopt structural explanations of inequitable power arrangements in the home and public sphere to explain difficulties faced by women. A critical theorist in anthropology might lobby for greater political opportunity for a cultural group that is disenfranchised by the political system.

Another type of structuralism is **institutionalism**. While many structuralists devise explanations concerning social and power structures that are "deeply embedded" within our cultures, institutionalists look at the more visible interactions between people and the institutions

---

5. The relative influence of "rational choice" versus structural factors in human decision making has broad philosophical and political ramifications. Rational choice analysis may take into account "structural"-type factors but ultimately suggests that individual decision making and "free will" determine outcomes, while structuralists view opportunity structures as creating more "determinist"-type outcomes for decision makers.

that govern them. Many of the guiding principles of the "founding fathers" of the United States were institutionalist and predicated on the belief that good institutions would constrain the worst instincts of human behavior.

Behavioralism, Positivism, and Realism: Inductive Midlevel Analysis

Rather than deductively positing the presence of top-down forces that influence society, as is the case with **macrolevel theory**, midlevel theorists examine breakdown causality into a set of separate potential causes, each of which is investigated in turn. **Midlevel theory** often uses statistics to analyze a small number of potential causes over larger numbers of cases to determine which tend to be best related to outcomes.

The focus of midlevel theorists on observable data suggests that causal factors, which are unseen, are not as easily understood under this framework. In the social sciences, the tradition of *behavioralism* is associated with the midlevel traditions, in particular. The term indicates that the outward, observable behavior of individuals is the appropriate focus of study rather than their inner, unobservable, decision-making processes. Theoretical inferences, however, are built on inductive intuition to a large degree, an approach that researchers in other traditions sometimes find less theoretically rich or rigorous.

Midlevel data are obtained either experimentally (which will be discussed in a later chapter) or through inductive observation and research. Ontologically, midlevel theorists are largely guided by a *positivist* understanding of the world. Positivism views the world as full of objective "things" that can be studied and measured. Others suggest that the assumptions underlying a positivist perspective are too strong and that natural and social sciences actually tend to be guided by principles of *realism*. Realism, as an epistemological term, suggests that, while not everything is observable, there are many objective facts that can be partly understood through repeated analysis and study (see Shapiro, 2005).

The benefit of midlevel research lies in its ability to create theory whose propositions are ultimately testable. Not surprisingly, it represents the mainstream in many scholarly traditions in both the natural and social sciences. The downside is reflected in the shortcomings of all quantitative research, namely, the frequent sacrifice of theoretical detail in the search for and use of quantifiable data.

Building a Theoretical Argument

Developing theories to explain causal processes lies at the heart of research. However, theoretical development is useless to others unless it is presented as a **theoretical argument**. By argument, I simply mean how and whether causality is inferred and presented in a convincing manner. Theoretical arguments do not rest on rhetoric, but, rather, the strength of the methodologies, underlying assumptions, logical connections, and the elimination of alternate theories.

Deductive Argumentation:
Syllogisms, Conditional Logic, and Mathematics

Deductive arguments flow from assumptions or axioms. These assumptions are not justified in terms of how they were made or what measurable evidence supports them. Deductive reasoning is only valid when the assertion of the conclusion is necessarily supported by these starting assumptions. How then, does one make a causal argument that leads from assumption to conclusion?

Deductive argumentation can be very dense, involving page after page of symbolic logic and mathematics. In other cases, a series of brief statements are all that are involved. In either case, an audience is asked to go along with the assumptions underlying the argument connecting initial premises to causal conclusion.

Two basic kinds of logical argumentation involved in deductive reasoning involve the use of **syllogisms** and **conditional logic**. Syllogisms take the form of (a) a major premise, which defines what does or does not belong to a group; (b) a minor premise, which describes whether or not something is considered a subset of an element of the group; and (c) a concluding argument that establishes whether the item described in (b) actually belongs to the group defined in (a). Since all that writing is difficult to wrap one's mind around, we turn to an example of a syllogism that employs symbols:

All X are Y

Z is X

Therefore, Z is Y.

Fill in the Xs, Ys, and Zs, and you get examples like the following:

All politicians lie

George is a politician

Therefore, George is a liar.

Few theories in the social sciences are built around the determinist logic of syllogism. Conditional logic, however, tends to be a much more common approach. Conditional logic, as the name implies, is based less on absolutes and more on outcomes that are expected to occur under certain conditions. Outcomes can occur with certainty under certain conditions or they can happen sometimes, or they can occur probabilistically. The "IF–THEN" nature of conditional logic opens the door to empirical verification that establishes whether or not the statement holds up under observation. At the same time, **counterfactual reasoning** suggests what would occur in "imaginary" cases if the logic were not true. Such counterfactual reasoning might not be empirically verifiable, but it still represents an important tool in deductive arguments that purport to explain a single or a limited number of causal events. As Fearon (1991) clarifies, "The analyst in explaining why event E occurred, cannot help but explain why E occurred *rather than* some other possible outcome or outcomes" (p. 172).

Most of the deductive arguments found in the natural sciences are conditional. IF this is true . . . THEN this can also be expected to be true. In the social sciences, conditional logic is found in game theory and other formal attempts to model human behavior. For humanities scholars, the focus might not be on measurable concepts, but the logic of argumentation found in conditional logic remains the same.

Although deductive arguments may be made "in plain English" through syllogisms or conditional statements, the use of mathematics in clarifying causal relationships is commonplace. Mathematics is simply a symbolic way of expressing logical, albeit often complex, relationships.

Mathematics might be used to help understand regular patterns of interaction, whether among molecules or among people. Of course, no matter how complicated the math, a researcher's entire theoretical edifice rests on the assumptions that go into the equations. Defending challengeable assumptions is an important part of theory building, particularly where deductive reasoning is involved.

Inductive Argumentation: Four Steps for Building a Convincing Argument

Unlike deductive reasoning, researchers building a theory inductively must weigh various types of evidence in inferring causal relations from the observed world. This weight-of-the-evidence approach might appear to lack the rigor that deductive reasoning offers, but, at the same time, frees the researcher from the need to begin with rigorous assumptions that can oversimplify reality. Due to the lack of guiding assumptions, however, building a theory from the ground up presents serious challenges. Below I offer some tips to help simplify the process of "messy" inductive theorizing. These steps are as follows.

Step 1: Situate the Emerging Theory Within the Larger Body of Research

For many researchers,[6] the first stage of theory building, whether inductive or deductive, often involves conducting a **literature review** to help derive a research question and better understand how it differs from and/or extends on similar types of projects conducted in the past. A researcher wants to know how the question fits into the big picture, what differentiates it from similar questions, and how other efforts inform the causal story being developed. Once this occurs, the researcher can approach his or her own causal theory having weighed the evidence of other research first. Inadequate review of previous research leads to wasted effort, resources, and, in fields such as medicine, even the loss of lives.

It can be useful to differentiate the process of reviewing literature at this stage of theory building from the formalized literature review as it is reported in a research paper or book at the end of a project. The "process of reviewing literature" at the beginning (and throughout) of a paper provides a researcher with an understanding of the causal relationships uncovered or argued by others and guides his or her search for novel understandings. The final "literature review section" of a written work, which may not be labeled explicitly as such, is where the researcher relays to the reader what the findings of other researchers were and argues why his or her research is useful in refuting, clarifying, or extending previous efforts. Usually organized thematically or chronologically, a written literature review is the end product of a process of theoretical framing that often begins at the outset of a project. An example is found in the appendix found at the end of Chapter 2.

Step 2: Identify Variables, Establish Their Correlation, and Argue Causality

Attempting to understand causal relations inductively often results in a certain degree of "information overload." By the time a researcher

---

6. Some researchers, on the other hand, object to conducting a literature review at the outset of a project. Glaser (1978), for example, suggests that reviewing literature in the field can contaminate a researcher's thinking and prevent him or her from coming up with original ideas. Such researcher's do not reject reviewing literature altogether, only doing so as the first step.

attempts to devise a causal theory, he or she should have attempted to tame the subject matter to a certain extent through the process of conceptualization and classification. This allows for the analysis of manageable categories of different explanatory factors and outcomes. Identifying these categories of analysis, or variables, is the first important step in building a theory.

To establish a causal theory, one must establish that a change in some variables is associated with a change in others. Only when such a correlation can be shown to exist can a researcher move forward with suggestions concerning causal relationships. Correlation is, in principle, a necessary precondition to causality.

Correlations can be statistical, such as the presence of lower levels of violent crimes in U.S. states lacking the death penalty. They can also be qualitative, like the observation that higher employee morale accompanied the institution of a new dental plan at a company. In the first instance, the correlation exists between a variable representing different crime rates and one indicating whether a state has or does not have a death penalty. In the second instance, a correlation exists between one variable reflecting the level of employee morale and the other whether or not a dental plan was in place. In neither of these examples, however, can one infer a causal relationship solely based on the presence of a correlation between variables.

The phrase "correlation does not equal causation" has become a well-worn cliché among academics. There are two major reasons why correlations might be deceptive. The first involves the influence of an omitted (aka a confounding or lurking) variable. Oftentimes, two variables might seem to be associated but only move in tandem because they are both related to a third (or more) variable. For instance, in the example of workers' morale increasing when a dental plan was instituted, it might be possible that a pay raise was instituted at the same time as the dental plan. The increase in morale might therefore be related to the pay raise rather than any increase in benefits. The conclusion that increasing benefits affects morale is based on a **spurious relationship**. The centrality of the omitted variable problem for research will be discussed further in Chapter 4.

Even more deceptive is the role that time itself can play as a confounding variable. Two unrelated variables, for instance, might increase or decrease over time. Numerically speaking, poverty rates and the number of male nurses have been correlated in the United States in recent years, even though there is no causal connection. The correlation is deceptive because a third variable—the passage of time—is correlated with each of these unrelated phenomena.

Another reason that equating correlation with causation is perilous involves the directionality of the causal relationship. Even if a causal relation between variables exists, the fact that a correlation exists says nothing about how the variables relate. Does variable *A* influence variable *B*, or vice versa? Or, do they influence each other at the same time in whole or in part?

Establishing the basic direction of causality is an important challenge. The simplest and most convincing way to do this is to show that changes in one variable precede changes in another variable (known as the "antecedent principle"). If, for instance, changes in death penalty laws tend to precede changes in violence rates, then there is more evidence for a causal relationship than if the correlation is examined only at a given point in time.

All is not lost if the temporal ordering of variable changes cannot be established. However, the need for a convincing cause-and-effect argument on other grounds becomes even stronger. Sometimes cause-and-effect relationships can be understood through common sense. For instance, all other things being equal, it's hard to imagine lung cancer leading to smoking, rather than the other way around. Other times, subsequent experiments and statistical methods can help better establish the direction of a relationship.

Even if a researcher answers basic questions concerning the causal direction of the variables of interest, the central question of theory concerns *why* things happen as they do. Hopefully, through the process of observation and the basic analysis of primary data, a researcher has gleaned a measure of insight into the causal mechanisms that are occurring. If so, then the researcher can further develop the causal inferences he or she has collected and develop a "plausible story" of causality.

Step 3: Eliminate Alternate Explanations

Almost any causal story can be explained in terms other than those offered by the researcher. Part of the process of reviewing literature described in Step 1 involves identifying these alternate explanations. Other times, it is up to the researcher to identify these potential alternate explanations, even if no one else has offered them. For an inductive theory to represent the *most* plausible explanation of a phenomenon, other plausible explanations need to be evaluated.

For example, in the classic sociological text, *On Suicide*, the famous early sociologist Émile Durkheim couples persuasive argumentation with the use of correlational statistics to eliminate alternate causal theories such as the influence of psychological disorders, alcoholism, and climatic differences before asserting his causal theory linking societal factors to suicide. Like a doctor isolating an illness, inductive theory building is most effective when causality is increasingly narrowed to one explanation.

One convincing way in which researchers eliminate alternate theories is through *comparative methodologies*. "Comparativists" are common in many fields. From linguistics to law, from history to biology, researchers studying a variety of issues do so comparatively. Comparative studies offer a strong framework for theoretical development by eliminating alternative theories through the careful selection of cases in small sample, qualitative research (Table 3.1).

Statements about causality are often somewhat speculative but are especially tenuous when many factors might account for the outcome of just a handful of events. This problem involving "many variables and few cases" was recognized by the English philosopher John Stuart Mill, who offered approaches to help better determine which factors were most important in determining outcomes.

Mill's best known logical formulations for dealing with small-n research were his Method of Agreement and Method of Difference. Each method seeks to eliminate alternate explanations in order to arrive at a

Table 3.1:   Comparative Methodology Designs

	Most Similar Case Designs	*Most Different Case Designs*
Casual Factors (Independent Variables)	Mostly the same	Mostly different
Outcomes (Dependent Variables)	Mostly different	Mostly the same

single causal factor responsible for outcomes. The Method of Agreement suggests that if a different outcome is witnessed in two or more cases that are dissimilar in every way but one, then that outcome occurs due to the factor they have in common. Mill's Method of Agreement is used in modern theoretical research that employs what are now known (somewhat confusingly) as *most different case* (or system) *designs*.

The Method of Difference suggests that if two or more cases are similar in every way except one and a different outcome is observed, then the outcome is attributable to the factor in which they differed. Mill's Method of Difference underlies the research design of most theory-oriented comparative projects. This is probably because it is usually easier to establish that two cases are mostly similar than mostly different and because it is more difficult to argue causal inferences when there is no variance in outcomes. In the social sciences, the principles of Mill's Method of Difference underlie what are called "*most similar case* (or system) *designs*."

Most similar case designs seek to build theory inductively by examining similar examples that differ in small number of ways and attempting to isolate the relevant causal factors. Underlying this method is the (extremely important) idea of *controlling* for extraneous factors—holding things constant that are not of theoretical interest. For instance, Anckar (2004) studies why some countries instituted the death penalty when others didn't by comparing as part of his study, similar countries that nevertheless varied in terms of their socioeconomic status, religion, and history. He then builds a theory based, in large part, on the role that religion and a history of slavery played in modern-day support for capital punishment.

Case selection is the most important aspect of the entire enterprise when it comes to small-scale comparative studies that are conducted for the purposes of building theory. Case selection generally entails finding similar settings and time periods for comparison. For instance, let's say an education researcher were developing a theory that different graduation rates in high schools were attributable to the differing curriculum of those schools. To eliminate competing explanations, it would be better to select two schools with different curriculum and graduation rates, but otherwise similar attributes, for example, two inner-city schools rather than an inner-city school and a suburban school, for the purposes of the study.

The most ideal most similar designs are often those that examine a similar setting but during different time periods when some attribute of that setting changed. For most given settings, it is likely that most things will stay the same over the short and medium term. For instance, a given high school will have similar enrollments, teachers, and budgets from one year to another. So, if a new curriculum is instituted, and graduation rates change noticeably from one year to the next, it is more likely that the curriculum was responsible for the change than other factors that stayed largely constant.

Most similar designs offer theories that are more likely to withstand scrutiny than ones in which cases are selected in an ad hoc manner, even if the arguments that are developed are far from foolproof. By controlling for a variety of other factors, most similar case designs effectively discredit many alternate explanations of causality other than the explanation offered by the researcher.

Step 4: Consider the Deductive Implications

The term *deductive* is confusing, because it really implies two things for research. The focus thus far has been on arriving at a causal theory through abstract reasoning based on nonempirical assumptions. Deductive reasoning, also, however, implies the ability to move from theory toward the empirical verification of the theory's conclusions.

Many research projects simply end with a theoretical argument and may not be verifiable. This is particularly true of qualitative theories that infer causality in a unique circumstance. The best that can be done in these cases is a kind of trial-and-error application to real-world situations to see whether the theory seems to offer a plausible understanding of what is happening. Other theories, such as macrolevel structural theories, may also be difficult to apply to empirical circumstances.

In cases where examining the applicability of the theory to the empirical world is plausible, a "switch" from inductive to deductive language occurs as a researcher explains his or her theory. Oftentimes, such theories employ logical connectors to explain IF something is true THEN this is what we would expect to see. Such a theoretical argument includes the empirical implications of the theory. If the theory is correct, then what would be witnessed in a similar situation? The "scientific method" itself suggests a "switch" from inductive observation to the deduction of empirical hypotheses in its organizational framework,[7] which begins with observation and then proceeds to hypothesis formulation and testing.

---

7. There is actually no one agreed-on scientific method, even if the general steps are the same in different versions. The fact that such a famous methodological framework has numerous versions reflects that methodological specifics are often interpreted in various ways.

Conclusion

The main point of this chapter was to explore different approaches that researchers take to make causal arguments. There are broad traditions in theory building that include whether to approach causality inductively or deductively and whether or not the causal analysis might be described as a quantitative trend; a more contextual, qualitative phenomenon; or both. I discussed theoretical levels of analysis as divided into macro-, mid-, and microtheories and provided examples of different social science approaches that illustrate these levels combined with a description of their inductive or deductive nature. These examples included interpretivist, rational choice, structuralist, ethnographic, and behavioralist traditions. I concluded with some suggestions about how a researcher might best go about building inductive and deductive theories.

DISCUSSION QUESTIONS

3.1 Which of the following passages is inductive? Which is deductive? Why? Why might each conclusion be faulty?

a. The last two wars fought by the United States were in the Middle East. Much of the world's oil is found in the Middle East. The United States fights its wars over oil.
b. The number of severe hurricanes has increased in recent years in the Western Atlantic. Hurricane intensity can be affected by ocean temperatures. Ocean temperatures can be affected by global warming. The number of hurricanes has increased in recent years due to global warming.

3.2 Come up with a research question that might be considered "descriptive." Now, turn that question into one that involves causality. Did you need to answer the descriptive question before addressing causal ones?

3.3 Unlike factual, descriptive information, causality, whether in the social or natural sciences, can never be "proven." Why?

3.4 How do researchers go about making arguments about causality? What problems do researchers encounter that might mislead them into drawing false causal conclusions? What role does methodology play in helping researchers to overcome these problems?

3.5 Come up with one research question that might be asked in the humanities and two research questions, one more qualitative and one more quantitative, that might be asked in the social sciences. Would the methodologies involved in addressing the humanities question be similar to those involved in addressing the quantitative social science question?

3.6 What are the advantages of qualitative research versus quantitative research and vice versa? How do we know what the best type of project to conduct is?

3.7 Come up with a research question that would entail research that combines qualitative and quantitative research. How would such research improve on research that only used one type of approach or the other?

3.8 Think about an important historical event. How could we use micro-, mid-, and macrolevels of analysis to best understand what happened? What types of causal explanations are most important at each level?

Appendix to Chapter 3

Prisoner's Dilemma:
A Simple Example of Formal, Rational Choice Theory

During the 1950s, Merill M. Flood, Melvin Dresher, and Albert W. Tucker famously derived a model known as "prisoner's dilemma" that has informed the expectations of generations of social scientists attempting to understand why it is difficult to reach binding agreements between mutually self-interested parties. The name derives from the sample situation of two prisoners captured for the same crime who, without the ability to coordinate with one another, are given two choices: (1) inform on one's accomplice or (2) keep silent in the hope that the other prisoner will as well.

Given the two potential choices, a theorist wants to understand how each prisoner will behave (his or her "strategy") in order to achieve the best outcome for himself or herself, in this case meaning the smallest amount of prison time (notice already that rational choice is based on assumptions like the number and nature of the choices available and the motivations of the "players"). The less prison time a prisoner receives, the higher the "utility" of the outcome for that prisoner. Thus, each prisoner will attempt to choose the strategy that minimizes prison time while maximizing utility.

Based on the two choices given to each prisoner, there are four possible outcomes to our simple prisoner's dilemma: (1) Prisoner 1 informs on Prisoner 2 while Prisoner 2 informs on Prisoner 1, (2) Prisoner 1 informs on Prisoner 2 while Prisoner 2 stays silent, (3) Prisoner 1 stays silent while Prisoner 2 informs on Prisoner 1, or (4) both prisoners stay silent.

Depending on each outcome, each prisoner receives an amount of utility that I will call 4, 3, 2, and 1, with 4 representing the best outcome for a prisoner (highest utility, least prison time), 1 the worst outcome, and 3 and 2 in the middle in descending order of utility. The numbers in this example aren't meaningful except that we know that $4 > 3 > 2 > 1$, whatever each represents.

Given the assumed choices, outcomes, and utilities, Prisoner's dilemma is modeled thus, with each square listing the utility of each outcome for Prisoner 1 followed by the utility for Prisoner 2:

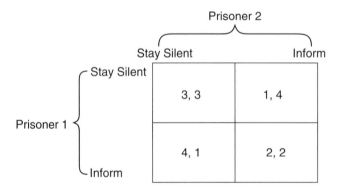

A model of Prisoner's Dilemma

The key to understanding the expected outcome (in this case called a "Nash equilibrium") is to analyze how a rationally self-interested prisoner would act given his or her expectations of the actions of the other prisoner. In this case, the expected outcome would be that each prisoner would inform on one another.

Why? Examining the outcomes, it becomes clear that no matter what the other prisoner does, it is always in the self-interest of a prisoner to choose the "inform" option. Prisoner 1, for instance, obtains "4" utility (immunity from prosecution, for example) if he or she informs on Prisoner 2 if Prisoner 2 keeps silent while only obtaining a "3" for keeping silent while Prisoner 2 keeps silent (maybe they will still be successfully prosecuted). On the other hand, if Prisoner 2 informs on Prisoner 1, Prisoner 1 will still want to inform on Prisoner 2. Rather than playing the "patsy" and keeping silent (utility = 1), Prisoner 1 will also want to inform on Prisoner 2 and hope to obtain some goodwill from the authorities (utility = 2). The point of the exercise is to show that the suboptimal outcome of both prisoners informing on one another (2, 2), rather than keeping silent (3, 3), is what one would expect as a result of both prisoners behaving to maximize self-interest.

The prisoner's dilemma model is used to help explain actors behave in contexts such as those involving trade agreements or arms control treaties when the benefits of individual defection prevent the achievement of collectively good outcomes. A variety of conditions can be added to make the model more sophisticated such as the addition of choices, strategies, institutional restrictions, and expectations of repeated interactions.

Prisoner's dilemma is itself only illustrative of a tiny part of the vast and varied types of undertakings of formal, rational choice theorists. The purpose in using the example has been to show how predictions of human behavior can be deduced through a set of assumptions that dictate logical outcomes.

PART III

Verifying Theory

4

Preparing to Test Hypotheses

Overview

This chapter identifies the steps that a researcher takes in preparing to test quantitative-type theories through empirical analysis. It discusses how models and hypotheses are deduced from theories and how data are created through processes of **operationalization** and **experimentation**.

In discussing operationalization, the discussion introduces a **typology** of different variables used in quantitative research. Furthermore, discussion looks at the terms *validity*, *reliability*, and *precision*, and shows how such terms are used somewhat differently when discussing research design versus variable measurement.

The chapter concludes with an extended discussion of the benefits of experimental data collection over simple nonexperimentally collected observational data. It examines the steps in a "classic experimentation" and describes how they overcome specific methodological issues involving omitted variables, causal simultaneity, and measurement errors.

Introduction

The term *theory* connotes a certain degree of uncertainty. Deductively derived theories often rest on questionable assumptions, while inductively derived theories rest on a researcher's ability to weigh evidence successfully. All theories, however, are not equally uncertain. Some are tentative, others are well established. Most are somewhere in-between. What determines how much credibility a theory is lent by scholars?

A theory's credibility increases as additional information is gathered that accords with the predictions of the theory's propositions. Researchers test hypotheses by assessing the generalizability of their original assertions. If the researcher's theory is purely qualitative and contextual, therefore, then empirical verification through quantitative testing is impossible. In Chapters 5 and 6, I discuss how researchers seek to verify their theories by collecting further empirical information and seeing if it conforms to theoretical expectations.

If a researcher is conducting quantitatively oriented research with the goal of assessing hypotheses, then there are numerous intermediary steps lying between successfully building a theory and empirically testing its assertions. First, researchers must pare down their theories into models and use these models to help them create hypotheses about proposed relationships between variables. Second, if researchers do not have quantitative data available for testing, then they have to collect additional information, often through operationalization and experimentation.

Operationalization is an extension of conceptualization and involves assigning numerical values to latent variables. The process of operationalization is guided by the standards of validity, reliability, and precision— each of which is discussed at length later in this chapter. Experimentation, which plays a major role in data collection in the natural sciences and social sciences fields such as psychology, allows researchers to collect data that are more useful than those obtained through simple observation.

Before discussing issues involved with models, hypotheses, operationalization, and experimentation, however, it is useful to start with a basic discussion of variables. Up to this point, I have used the term *variable* sparingly to avoid its connotative association with quantitative analysis. Variables, however, are the basic unit of statistical testing, just as words are the basic units of language. Just as words can be divided into categories such as nouns, verbs, adjectives, adverbs, and interjections, variables may be divided into different types.

A Typology of Variables

All things in the universe are either constant or variable. Constants are things that only take on one value, like the speed of light or the value of π. Variables can take on anything from two to an infinite number of different values. Looking around the room, you can observe the current value taken by lots of variable—How much light is the lamp emitting? How many chairs are in the room? What is the room temperature? All these things may take on different values in different rooms, which is what makes them "variable." There are two things that interest a researcher about variables: (1) the kinds of values taken by a particular variable and (2) how the values of different variables relate to one another. Both of these questions influence how variables are used in modeling and statistical testing.

In evaluating the characteristics of different kinds of variables, researchers begin with the understanding that different types of variables take on different types of values. The most basic divide is between **continuous** and **discrete variables**. Continuous variables take on all values within a given range, including every possible decimal, while discrete variables take on only certain values.

Continuous variables are numbers that are infinitely subdivisible. Examples include people's weights and heights. A person's weight could be measured in kilogram, gram, milligram, nanogram, and so on, while a person's height could be measured in meters, centimeters, millimeters, and so on.

Discrete variables represent every other type of variable that is not continuous and can be understood as divisible into two categories: quantitative and categorical. **Discrete quantitative variables** are similar to continuous variables in the sense that they represent something that is numerically conceptual but only as a whole number. "Counts," often of things such as events, such as the number of protests in different cities or countries, are discrete quantitative variables. So too would the number of pets people own. Neither protests nor pets could be sensibly represented as a fraction, although each is clearly a number (see Figure 4.1).

Categorical (or qualitative) variables are, on the other hand, nonquantitative discrete variables. Categorical variables take on values that are not measurable as numbers. While a person's height might be measured as a continuous variable and the number of eyes they have as a discrete quantitative variable, the color of their eyes would represent a categorical variable. Other categorical variables might include a person's political party, the phases of the moon, or different historical epochs. Categorical variables can also express a sense of order (**ordinal variables**) such as slow, fast, and fastest. Variables with no sensible ordering are known as **nominal variables**. The importance of understanding the different types of variables will become clearer in Chapter 5.

Finally, researchers are interested not only in the characteristics of particular variables but also in their relationship to one another. Once a researcher begins developing a causal theory, he or she can begin to speak of causal factors as **independent variables** and observed or

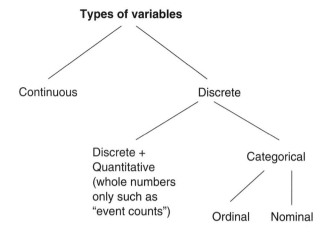

Figure 4.1:   Breakdown of individual variable types

expected outcomes as **dependent variables**. The terms *independent* and *dependent* variables only have meaning in relation to one another. A variable itself, absent a suggested relation to another variable, cannot be described as either (see Table 4.1).

Most research projects seek to ascertain how multiple independent variables effect changes in the values of dependent variables. However, since the causal relationship between variables is generally intangible, it can be debatable whether or not a researcher is correct in his or her assignment of the terms *independent* and *dependent*.

Theoretical Models

Variables represent the building blocks of theories and are central to models that arise from those theories. Even when the word *variable* is not expressly used in conjunction with theory building, the relationship between independent and dependent variables is implicitly being explored. When it comes to simplifying theories into models, the terminology of variables becomes even more important. Theoretical models summarize the relationships among variables that are believed to affect one another causally.

The term *model*, of course, is used in a variety of contexts. The broadest definition of models used in research suggests that they denote simplified representations of things or processes. Models are built to depict the most important features that affect performance or outcome.

Table 4.1:   Examples of Independent and Dependent Variables

Independent Variables	Dependent Variables
Whether or not someone is homeless	How many calories a day someone consumes
Number of cigarettes smoked	Likelihood of becoming ill
Amount of education before age 30	Salary at age 60
Parents' political party affiliation	Likelihood of voting for a particular party in an election
Examples in which it is less clear which is the independent and which is the dependent variable	
Arrest rates in city neighborhoods	Crime rates in city neighborhoods
How democratic a country is	Economic growth rates in a country
Levels of illegal drug or alcohol consumption	Whether or not someone has psychological problems

While theories might discuss at great length how causality is under-stood to work, the main point of most models is simply to express the interrelationships between variables in a theory. Since models are based on the assumptions of theory, they are a deductive step that, along with hypotheses, bridges the gap between theories and what a researcher expects to witness in the empirical world.

Models are often presented as graphical or mathematical representa-tions. When presented graphically, models generally use arrows to show the direction and connections between independent and dependent vari-ables. Figure 4.2 shows a simple example of a graphical model.

Mathematical models take many forms, but when depicting causality, most start by depicting independent variables as "$x's$" and a singular dependent variable as "y," and then specifying, through the rest of equa-tion, how y might be expected to change as the "$x's$" change. Mathematical models have the disadvantage of being less easily decipher-able than graphical ones to the average reader, but they have the advan-tage of being more directly amenable to testing through using the statistical operations described in Chapter 5.

One example of a model might be one constructed by a political fore-caster that identifies several independent variables, such as the unem-ployment rate, presidential approval, or amount of national cloud cover,

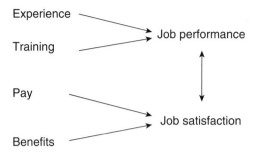

Figure 4.2:   Sample graphical model

and uses them to predict the outcome of a future presidential election. One can assume that each of the variables used has some sort of theoretical underpinning; they were not simply pulled from a hat. Each of the independent variables would be weighted in some way and a relationship with the dependent variable (election outcome) determined based on a researcher's theory and data obtained from past elections. If information about the independent variables successfully predicts the outcome of the election, then the model could be credibly used as a tool to predict future elections and elections in other places.

The most important thing about models is that they are simpler and more convenient to work with than potentially dense causal theories. It is easier for a researcher, or other researchers, to understand, work with, and "tweak" an explicitly expressed model of causal relationships than it is to do the same with the underlying theory on which the model is based. Furthermore, models clearly display theoretical relationships that might be tested empirically. If the relationships depicted in a model are borne out through further empirical investigation, then the model can be said to be predictive. The famous economist Milton Friedman (1953) famously argued that the predictive value of a model even supersedes in importance the underlying theoretical assumptions that the model is based on. Whether one agrees with the assertion or not, successful models provide a framework for testing the propositions of a theory.

Hypotheses

The term **hypothesis**, like many other terms in research methodology, is often used informally in everyday language. If I were to ask students in an introductory methodology class how to define the word, I would almost certainly receive the response "an educated guess" from a large number of students. This definition suffices for informal situations of uncertainty in everyday life but is inadequate for describing the role that hypotheses play in analytical research. While the outcome of hypotheses is uncertain, the word *guess*, no matter how educated, fails to capture how hypotheses are derived. A better definition for the term *hypothesis* is that it is more of an "expectation" one would expect to see if the causal relationships suggested by a theory are correct.

It is best to think of hypotheses as conjectures that arise from, rather than lead to, causal theory. Theories are inferred, while hypotheses are deduced from the inferred theoretical relationships. Hypotheses serve as a bridge from theories (or models) to the further analysis of empirical data. Researchers use hypotheses to point the way to future analysis by suggesting what relationship should exist between concepts/variables whose relationship has already been specified (see Figure 4.3).

Figure 4.3:   Hypotheses: Bridging theory and evidence

It is also important not to confuse the usage of the term *hypothesis* with that of a *research question*. Research projects begin with open-minded inquiry into a subject matter—a question or set of questions to be asked. Hypotheses are inappropriate bases for initiating a research agenda because they suggest a preconceived notion of outcomes in the absence of research evidence. This can only bias future research effort, as a researcher, knowingly or unknowingly, is likely to collect evidence supporting his or her preconceptions while ignoring or disregarding evidence to the contrary.

Hypotheses are usually stated in a conventional format. They are, or at least tend to be

- definitively worded statements that
- link two concepts/variables by indicating something about the
- direction or existence of the relationship between the variables.

An example would be as follows: The older someone becomes, the less likely he or she is to act aggressively. This hypothesis would have been deduced from a theory that explained the inferred causal linkage between age and aggression.

After the hypothesis is specified, it would be necessary to find a way to test it. The entire point of formulating hypotheses is to specify the empirical conditions that would verify or discount particular theoretical assertions. To test the hypothesis linking age to aggression mentioned above, however, a researcher would have to quantify, or operationalize, aggression in some manner. The next section discusses issues involving the operationalization and measurement of such intangible concepts.

Operationalization and Measurement

Social scientists, more than natural scientists, have to find ways to measure intangible concepts so that they might be better understood and tested. Social scientists have made great strides in recent decades in their efforts to quantify difficult variables such as power, student performance, mental disorders, or, in one noteworthy case, romantic love.

In a 1970 study, the psychologist Zick Rubin devised a questionnaire that surveyed the feelings that undergraduate couples felt toward one another. He also placed pairs of undergraduates in a room and observed them behind a two-way mirror, stopwatch in hand, and recorded the total amount of time they spent gazing at one another. By mathematically analyzing the answers given on the questionnaire, he found that a portion of the questions yielded answers that were not only strongly related to one another but also correlated with the amount of time the students spent looking at one another when they thought they were alone. If one accepts Rubin's use of "gazing time" as an accurate indication of the level of love the couples felt for one another, then he or she has devised a plausible way of measuring love through a simple set of questions.

Social scientists often seek to measure latent variables (or concepts, or constructs) in some credible way. Since the variables are latent, or intangible, there is no direct empirical way to "count" greater or lesser amounts in the same way that exists with more tangible phenomenon that would comprise most, if not all, variables in the natural sciences. Along with the comparative lack of experimentally derived data, the frequent use of latent variables is one of the single biggest differences between the natural and social sciences.

Oftentimes, cardinal numbers are meaningless when it comes to measuring underlying concepts. However, ordering greater or lesser amounts on scales is not. For instance, while most people can agree that some people have something called intelligence that is higher or lower for some people than other people, if an IQ (intelligent quotient) test reveals a score of a 100—what does the number 100 mean? The 100 represents an average score on a standardized scale, but in terms of units, it is not 100 of anything. Rather it is simply a score suggesting more "intelligence" than a score of 90 and less intelligence than 110.

Then there is the question of what IQ represents conceptually. Does it really measure intelligence, or something else? Would someone else measuring a particular person's intelligence get the same result using the same procedures? If not, how much would the results vary? Such questions were examined in the first chapter's discussion of conceptualization—but now we can discuss the same issues in light of the operational values that are derived. When assessing measurement issues, researchers use the terms *validity*, *reliability*, and *precision* to indicate greater or lesser accuracy of the measurements.

Validity, Reliability, and Precision: In Research Projects and in Measurement

Validity and **reliability** might be the two most common terms found in methodology books. The terminology can be confusing, however, because these terms are used in two distinct ways. The first way the terms are used as indicators of the quality of a research project as a whole—Can the entire project itself be described as being expected to yield valid and reliable results? Another way the terms are used is in dealing with the measurement of concepts—Does the operationalization process, that is to say the codification of different values of latent variables, yield values that are valid and reliable.

In both projects and specific measurements, definitions of validity and reliability indicate the same basic ideas. If something is *valid*, then what we are seeing best fits the answer to the underlying question. If we are speaking about research endeavors in their entirety, then the most valid way of answering our research question entails proceeding methodologically in a way that produces results that best answer the question.[1] If we are attempting to measure a latent concept, then the most valid measurement is the measurement most likely to reflect the nature of the underlying concept (see Figure 4.4).

Validity and Reliability in Research Projects

The validity of research projects is assessed in terms of "external" and "internal" validity. **External validity** represents the degree to which research findings obtained in one setting are applicable to other settings. For example, psychological researchers in a laboratory or other structured setting might witness completely different reactions from subjects than would occur in the outside world. While their research might be internally valid, any attempt to generalize about the research question would be biased by the setting in which the research was conducted.

Gerber and Green (2000), for instance, conducted an experiment involving different types of canvassing (mail, telephone, direct contact) on voter turnout in New Haven, Connecticut. While impressively designed "internally," one could question whether voters in New Haven would respond similarly to voters in another part of the country, or another country for that matter. To address such issues, the researchers have since expanded such research to other settings to determine whether the findings would remain consistent when the external validity of their project was expanded.

Internal validity, on the other hand, refers to the quality of the actual research process. Internal validity is threatened by both random, unsystematic as well as systematic methodological problems. Unsystematic threats to validity usually indicate methodological sloppiness—proceeding in a way that is unlikely to answer the question in a convincing manner. For example, if a researcher seeks to predict general public opinion solely through the use of a focus group, then there will be a disconnect between the question and the conclusions that are reached. *Bias*, on the other hand, is the systematic enemy of validity, and it is often difficult to

---

1. Throughout this chapter, I describe validity and reliability through the lens of *positivist-oriented* traditions. Other interpretations and uses of the word validity exist, however. Maxwell (1992, pp. 288–289), for instance suggests the term *interpretive validity* to describe the aim of interpretivist research in comprehending phenomena from the perspective of the participants in the situations being studied. Teddlie and Tashakkori (2003, p. 13) compile a list of 17 labels of different types of validity used in qualitative work. While many qualitative-interpretivists reject the use of the word "validity" entirely, the goal of successfully "capturing" reality, whether objective or subjectively conceived, is clearly a primary goal in all scholarship.

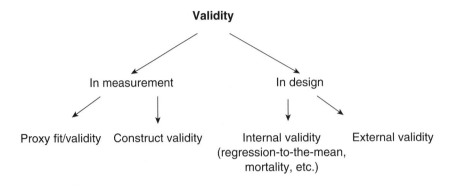

Figure 4.4: Breakdown of "validity"

detect. There are many examples of bias in research, but a few stand out as the most common.

Selection bias/unrepresentative case selection presents a problem when objects of a research study are not chosen randomly. Anytime anyone is paid to participate in a study, for instance, participants are more likely to be poorer than those not participating. For example, were a study of smoking conducted with paid volunteers, it is likely that the participants would be, on average, in worse health, regardless of the effects of smoking, than their financially better-off peers who did not participate. Since most qualitative studies involve studying a small, nonrandomly chosen selection of cases, the conclusions of such work must be interpreted with caution.

Selecting on the dependent variable is a potentially extreme source of bias in any project seeking to draw causal inferences. The denotation of this phrase is that a researcher will use values of the dependent variable to inform his or her choice of case selection (an acceptable practice). However, the common connotation of "selecting on the dependent variable" suggests that a researcher will only choose cases that have similar outcomes. While this is acceptable for exploratory research, usually no valid causal argument can be made about what causes something to happen without looking at cases in which it does not happen. For example, in literature exploring the causes of terrorism, it is common to examine the traits of convicted and suspected terrorists in order to see what they have in common. However, no one can convincingly link such common characteristics to a propensity for committing terrorist acts without examining nonterrorists to see if they lack those same traits.

Many other threats to internal validity exist as well. Sometimes, something external and uncontrollable happens in the middle of a project and influences subject responses. The pollution of the study in this manner is named (strangely, I think) **history**. Another source of bias known as **maturation** simply implies that something about the subjects themselves has changed during the course of a study in a way that might affect the results. **Mortality** on the other hand, rather than denoting (in many cases, at least) the death of study participants, simply indicates that the results of a study are brought into question when subjects drop out partway through for reasons that might be correlated with project outcomes.

The list of threats of internal validity goes on, but I will conclude this discussion by mentioning one of the most difficult ones for researchers, the idea of **regression to the mean**. Regression to the mean is a phenomenon that involves the tendency of extreme values that occur due to random chance to become less extreme over time. If a student takes a test and performs poorly one time and then improves on his or her score the next time, one might conclude that the student studied harder, understood the material better, and so on. However, it is also possible that a student performed poorly the first time because of random circumstances that were different from the second time the student took the test—perhaps the student got unlucky the first time by being asked the questions he or she was least prepared to answer, perhaps the student was sitting in front of someone with distracting sinus issues, or maybe the student himself or herself was feeling ill that day. All these random factors might account for the change in test score more than a change in ability.

By itself, regression to the mean is not a source of bias—it simply represents the behavior of extreme values in situations involving random factors. However, depending on how a researcher selects cases and attributes causation, a researcher can draw faulty conclusions.

Another example of regression to the mean occurs in the medical field, where it can be a central issue related to placebo effects. Placebo effects occur when those who are ill and receive medical treatment respond favorably, even if the treatment was ineffective. The phenomenon is often attributed solely to the power of suggestion that causes people to think they are better when they are not. However, because many medical conditions naturally strengthen and subside in intensity over time, some of the improvement experienced by the sickest of patients is undoubtedly a result of these patients regressing to the mean.

Having examined the concept of validity, what about reliability? Reliability is synonymous with "replicability." In many research projects, it is desirable to know that one researcher's work could be duplicated by another who would reach similar conclusions. In Chapter 2, I mentioned the example of scientists who claimed to have discovered "cold fusion" during the late 1980s. When their experiments were conducted by other researchers, however, no one obtained similar results. The lack of reliability of their work, in this case, was a tip-off to a lack of validity in their methods.

Research projects (as well as variable measurement) can, however, be reliable without being valid. Imagine that several researchers are all conducting their work based on the same set of faulty assumptions. They would reliably reach the same faulty conclusion, even if their research was not validly conducted. Climatologists, were in the past, for instance, accused of systematically utilizing temperature readings that were warmer than expected due to the proximity of measuring apparatuses to urban settings. Had this been true, it would have potentially affected the validity of climate research without necessarily affecting its reliability if such measurements had been a common practice.

Validity of Measurements

Validly measuring a variable means measuring it in a correct and convincing way such that there is minimal dispute as to whether a variable's values actually represent what is purportedly being measured. In the process of measurement, quantitative studies draw on different types of variables. Some variables are fairly clear-cut and can be measured either directly or almost directly through instruments. Other times, variables are conceptual in nature and can only be measured indirectly by anchoring intangible constructs to empirical referents. This process of *operationalizing* such concepts is challenging due to potential questions concerning validity and reliability that inevitably arise.

Sometimes people do not even realize that a variable is an operationalized concept. Wind chill factor is a good example. Unlike temperature, there is no straightforward way to measure wind chill. Wind chill measurements are primarily designed to capture how cold the interaction of temperature and wind actually feels to the average person. To measure the phenomenon as validly as possible, researchers established a set of empirical referents that could be measured and then combined into a single value. However, to do so, researchers had to make a set of assumptions including which direction a person faces (into the wind), the body part being affected (the face), and whether a person was walking or not (the assumption is 1.4 m/s). All of these assumptions can, of course, be challenged on the grounds that they do not validly represent what is being measured—namely, how cold it feels. Thus, even in natural sciences like meteorology, subjective discussions of conceptualization take place. In the case of wind chill, different countries use different measurements, and the National Weather Services of the United States and Canada both decided to overhaul their measurements of wind chill in 2001 to find a more valid representation of the concept.

One simple way of operationalizing a latent variable is to use an empirical *proxy variable* in its place. A proxy variable is a measurable variable that a researcher argues will respond similarly to other variables as the variable it represents. Such assumptions are often questionable at best. In one study, for example, Fearon and Laitin (2003) use the measurable variable "GDP [gross domestic product] per capita" as a proxy for the latent variable "state strength" in assessing the causes of civil conflict. However, one could easily argue that many poor countries, like North Korea, have strong states, while some rich countries have weak states. Proxy variables are convenient, but often questionable, shortcuts in operationalizing conceptual variables.

Whereas proxy variables and simple quantitative observational data denote **scalar variables** that represent measurements of only one thing, the conceptualization processes discussed in Chapter 2 can be extended and codified to create **composite variables**. Composite variables operationalize concepts by assigning values to the concepts that make up the variable and then combining them into a single variable.

Operationalizing composite variables is a more complex process than simply substituting a measurable variable for a latent variable such as is the case when using proxy variables. As with more complicated machines, more complicated processes of operationalization can be more useful, but there are also more things that can go wrong.

Validly measuring concepts actually entails three parts: (1) establishing that a variable has been conceptualized correctly and that the measurable subconcepts that make up the main concept are appropriate and appropriately related to one another, (2) establishing that the manner in which subconcepts (which are often proxy variables themselves) are measured is appropriate, and (3) aggregating the empirical measurements into a single "score" that is indicative of the main concept.

Let's again consider an earlier example, measuring intelligence. First, a researcher has to make the case for the appropriate elements that make up the concept—logical reasoning, spatial reasoning, and verbal reasoning would all be candidates. Once the researcher has made a case for the composition of intelligence, he or she would have to devise a way of measuring each of the elements that he or she has specified. Not only would the original specification of what makes intelligence have to be convincing, but the testing procedures for the different types of reasoning have to act as convincing empirical referents of those subconcepts. Last, the scores from the different tests would have to be combined with one another in some way so as to yield IQ scores that convincingly indicated different levels of intelligence.

Nowhere are the challenges presented by latent variables more evident than in the field of psychology. A familiar term for many readers is the term psychological construct. A major part of psychological research involves deciding what are and what are not the elements that make up personality profiles and disorders and how to measure them. There are, as a result, numerous terms derived from psychology (and now utilized throughout the social sciences) that specify how to assess whether or not constructs, or concepts, are convincingly reflecting what a researcher purports them to measure. Although methodologists sometimes disagree on the exact meaning of these terms, I offer the following typology of different types of measurement validity, as reflected in Figure 4.5.

Proxy Fit

As mentioned above, concepts may be operationalized either as simple proxies or as more intricate composite constructs. Simple proxy

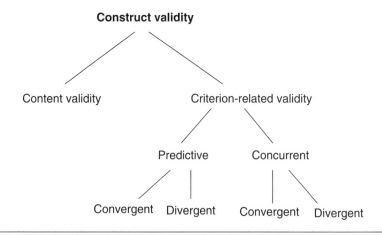

Figure 4.5: Breakdown of "construct validity"

measurements are often the simplest way to represent latent or undirectly measurable concepts. An example is global and regional climate conditions before the 1700s. One website (www.climatethoughts.org) lists 10 separate proxies that climatologists might use as measurable indicators of earlier climate conditions, such as ice cores, lake bed sentiments, pollen, and tree rings.

Of course, the main question a researcher wants to know about proxy variables involves how closely they match the concept that the researcher is attempting to measure. An attempt to asses proxy fit, for example, is found in a short article by Durden and Ellis (2003), who seek to understand whether class attendance at a university can be considered a proxy for student motivation. They find that the proxy is problematic and that student attendance and student motivation seem to have separate effects on exam performance. Convincing proxies can be hard to find in the social sciences, in particular, and the match between concept and proxy can rarely, if ever, be considered exact.

Construct Validity

As opposed to a proxy, researchers usually think of constructs/concepts as containing multiple elements. **Construct validity** is an overarching term that indicates the degree to which the conceptualization and measurement of such constructed variables corresponds with empirical reality.

There are two main ways to assess construct validity. First, we can analyze the process of conceptualization and determine if it has been done correctly. If so, then the concept is said to have **content validity**. Second, we could look at the end result—the measurements of a concept—and see how such measurements correlate with other empirical data that one would expect the measurements to correspond to. This is known as **criterion-related validity**.

Content Validity

There are two ways of approaching content validity—informally and formally. The informal approach is known as *face validity*. Face validity is one of the mushiest terms in the social sciences. It simply suggests that the breakdown of a concept "taken at face value" is valid and that proposed measurement procedures seem appropriate to the construct that it is intended to measure.

Formal assessment of content validity involves a more rigorous examination of conceptualization. This examination centers on assessing the same criteria for strong conceptualization discussed in Chapter 1. Is a concept broken down such that the categories constituting it are exhaustive but lack redundancy and are sensibly organized (nonconflated)? Are there irrelevant subconcepts?

A well thought-out assessment of content validity considers whether a strong theoretical case has been made for each part of the variable and how those parts fit together. However, there are statistical methods that aid in better establishing whether the content of constructs is sufficiently valid. Some modern methodologies are quite sophisticated, but the two most well-known methodologies are **interitem correlations** and **factor analysis**.

Interitem correlations simply involve correlating the values of each subcomponent of main concept and seeing whether or not each aspect is related to the others. For instance, a teacher might calculate the interitem correlations among different test sections to determine whether students are performing roughly similarly across different types of formats. Strong, positive correlations indicate that the concepts seem to fit together, whereas a variable that is only weakly related to others indicates that it probably does not belong in the conceptual framework. A correlation matrix can be created to quickly establish the bivariate correlations between several different measured variables. Although establishing correlation is particularly useful for latent variables built on indices of numerous measurable variables, correlational analysis itself will not help establish the relative weight of each measurable variable in relation to the main concept.

Factor analysis is a more sophisticated way of determining not only whether operational subconcepts fit well into the overall framework but also how strongly each should be "weighted" when considering their contribution to measurement of the conceptual variable as a whole. At the same time, the mathematical operations can help weed out redundant and irrelevant variables. While the details of factor analysis far exceed the purview of this work, the main point of such analysis is to mathematically group similar observed variables together in concepts according to their variance (exploratory factor analysis) or integrate latent variables into hypotheses testing procedures (confirmatory factor analysis, which is related to similar structural equation modeling). For those versed in such methods, conducting factor analysis provides the strongest arguments for the validity of conceptual content.

In Rubin's (1970) study on romantic love, which was mentioned earlier in this chapter, he used factor analysis to whittle down the questions provided on the student questionnaire from the original 80 questions to 13 questions that displayed the strongest variation with one another in terms of the answers provided. Those answers then, themselves, yielded a strong correlation to the amount of time students spent looking at one another behind the glass in the subsequent gazing experiment that he employed. Factor analysis is often used in such a fashion to group questions with similar answers together in research using questionnaires.

Criterion-Related Validity

Criterion-related validity considers the validity of a conceptual measurement by comparing it to the values of other variables. Unlike content validity, which considers the elements of a concept and how they are put together, criterion-related validity assesses a concept in terms of how it relates to other measured concepts. For example, if a test is devised to assess aggression in prison inmates, and the results correlate with the record of violent offenses for those inmates, it would indicate that a type of criterion-related validity exists.

Predictive validity examines how well the measurement of one latent variable can predict how another variable will behave in the future. A classic example is how well standard testing in high school predicts performance in college. If a test for college preparedness, such as the SAT (Scholastic Assessment Test) given in the United States, correlates strongly with a student's grades at the university, it could be said that the test has strong predictive validity. Along the same lines, **concurrent validity** examines how well the values of a measured latent variable correlate with a measure designed to measure the same concept at the same time. In this case, if a student receives similar relative scores on two tests taken at approximately the same time, such as the SAT and ACT, then there is evidence of concurrent validity.

Constructs assessed either predictively or concurrently are also assessed in terms of their **convergent** or **divergent validity**, which simply suggest the anticipated direction of the relationship between the main concept and the concept against which it is being assessed. If the values convincingly correlate in a positive direction, then convergent validity is said to exist, and if the values correlate negatively, then divergent or "discriminate" validity is said to exist. Depending on the expectations of a researcher, either may be evidence of construct validity.

Reliability of Measurements

As with the case in assessing research projects taken as a whole, measurement reliability suggests that subsequent researchers measuring the same variable (conceptual or directly empirical) should be able to arrive at the same measurements as previous researchers. Reliable measurement is particularly a concern when researchers use "judgment calls" in their operationalization of concepts.

For instance, when social scientists perform quantitative content analysis of documents, speeches, and other media, reliability is often a concern. As described in Chapter 2, content analysis is a descriptive form of research that involves "counting" words, phrases, and themes. Content analysis projects usually include a measure called "intercoder reliability." The higher the value, which is usually measured as either a percentage or correlation coefficient, the more faith the audience has that the data obtained can be trusted.

The same applies to all assessment of reliability. Data that cannot be replicated by other researchers is highly suspect when used for any type of further quantitative analysis. Ruggeri, Gizelis, and Dorussen (2011) call into question the common practice of "event coding" in international relations research by examining intercoder reliability within their own data set of United Nations interventions and finding serious problems related to "coder quality" as well as problems such as the tendency of coders to code simpler, more straightforward examples at the expense of more complex cases.

The visual aid most commonly utilized to display the relationship between validity and reliability is that of a target, with the bull's-eye in the middle representing the correct answer. Research or measurements that were valid and reliable would hit the bull's-eye every time. Research that was valid but not reliable would yield "holes" that circle the bull's-eye but never hit it. Research that was reliable but not valid can be represented by holes centered on some area of the target other than the bull's-eye. In the research world, when common procedures or common wisdom are wrong, multiple researchers can reach the same invalid conclusions (see Figure 4.6).

Precision of Measurements

If researchers pursue their research questions and measurements in a way that results center on the correct answer, then they are proceeding in a valid manner. Reliability indicates that their procedures can be replicated by future researchers. Precision suggests that researchers successfully zero in on correct answers with greater certainty.

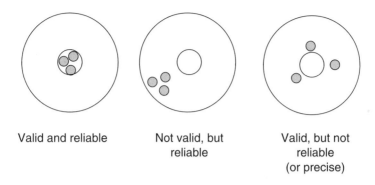

Valid and reliable | Not valid, but reliable | Valid, but not reliable (or precise)

Figure 4.6: Depiction of validity and reliability

The most common way to increase the amount of precision, whether in research as a whole or with a particular measurement, is to collect more data on the same subject. As more information about a subject is validly collected, the correct answer should, like puzzle pieces, form a clearer and clearer picture. The idea that more information is better is central, in particular, to statistical analysis, where it is known as the **law of large numbers**, which suggests that the average of numerous, validity-obtained, observations becomes closer to the true value of something as more observations are collected.

Consider, as a simple metaphor, the case of flipping a coin. If we are trying to find an answer to the question "how often does flipping a standard coin result in heads?" we could flip the coin five times. As long as the coin wasn't a trick coin or some other unusual circumstance, flipping a coin would be a valid and reliable way of answering the question. However, if we only flipped it five times, our answer wouldn't be very precise. There is no way it could even end up heads 50% of the time—the true answer. There is even a 1 in 32 chance that it would end up tails every time. However, what if we flipped it 50 times, or 500 times? In all likelihood, the percentage of times it ended up heads would be much closer to 50% than if we only flipped it five times. In this case, more information would yield a more precise answer to the research question.

Another issue that researchers often associate with precision is the scale at which variables are measured. Variables may be measured at a higher or lower scale that varies with the nature of the variable, how much information is known about the values it may take, and the goals of a researcher. While some variables naturally differ in terms of their "type," such as continuous and quantitative discrete variables, other times, researchers choose among different "levels of measurement."

Ratio measurements are the most precise variable scale and include continuous and quantitative discrete-type variables. Ratio measures describe variables as "normal numbers" that can be added, subtracted, divided, and multiplied in a meaningful way. The most important tip-off of a ratio variable is that zero indicates the absence of the thing being measured. For instance, weight is a ratio variable, because something that weighs zero kilograms actually weighs nothing.

Interval measurements or variables may, at first glance, appear to indicate normal numbers, but they do not. For such variables, the distance between the values has meaning, but they cannot be used in many types of mathematical operations because their value does not represent a traditional count of a number of things. In these cases, zero does not indicate the absence of the quantity being measured. Years and temperature, as they are traditionally measured, are both examples of interval variables. The year "zero" does not indicate the beginning of time on most calendars, and zero does not indicate the absence of temperature on either the Fahrenheit or Celsius scales.

Ordinal and *nominal* levels of measurement, which are both considered categorical variables, are less precise than interval measurements, because the distance between variable values no longer takes a set meaning. The values of ordinal values can be described in terms, at least, of whether or not they are higher or lower than one another. A good example of ordinal measurement would be the variable values obtained from a questionnaire employing a Likert scale, where answers tend to range from "strongly disagree" to "strongly agree." The preference ordering is clear, even though a number could not be meaningfully assigned to each answer, because the "distance" between each answer is unclear.

Nominal measurement, on the other hand, does not take values that can be described as greater or lesser than one another. Examples include types of cars, personal characteristics such as race, and political party affiliation. Unlike ordinal variables, which often could be measured more precisely, nominal variables tend to be naturally unquantifiable.

The simplest way to label a variable is as a **dichotomous variable**, which only takes two values. Gender is a common dichotomous variable, as is the answer to any yes-or-no question. When used for statistical calculations, dichotomous variables employ binary code, with 0s indicating one potential value of a variable and 1s indicating the other.

While some variables like gender are naturally dichotomous, measuring a variable dichotomously might be done for other reasons. The most common reason for a researcher to choose a less precise dichotomous measurement over a more precise ordinal, interval, or ratio measurement is because the researcher lacks detailed measurement concerning the values of a variable. When a dichotomous variable is used even though more detailed information is potentially available, the variable is known as a **dummy variable**.

For instance, let us say a researcher wants to assign a value to different countries indicating their majority religious affiliation. A continuous variable might assign a value to each percentage of the population but, given the lack of census data in many places, would likely be fraught with errors. A dichotomous variable, indicating simply whether or not a country was majority Christian, majority Muslim, and so on would be less precise but more likely to be correct. The famous economist John Maynard Keynes once said, "I'd rather be vaguely right, than precisely wrong." Oftentimes, this is exactly why researchers use less precise levels of measurement when more precise data might be available.

Experimental Data Collection

I conclude this chapter with a discussion of a methodology that is central to many research fields not only in the natural sciences but also in several of the social sciences. Experimentation is one of those terms that entire books have been written about. While particular methods associated with experimentation are varied and extensive, there are a few main points that tie together all classic experiments and the important role they play in creating data that researchers may subsequently analyze and use to infer causal conclusions.

Like many terms involved in research, "experiment" has both a commonly used connotation and a more specific usage for methodologists. The common understanding of an experiment is that something is being tested, as in "Let's do an experiment to see if this works." Methodologically speaking, however, an experiment is much more closely associated with information gathering than informational analysis.

Experimentation is an alternate form of data collection to that obtained through simple observation. With the exception of some qualitative studies involving participant observation, observational data collection is generally associated with a "hands-off" role on the part of the researcher. The researcher collects data but does not attempt to directly or indirectly influence the data being collected.

Experiments, on the other hand, depend on researcher intervention in guiding the data collection process. As with observational data collection, it is useful to think about experiments as serving either qualitative or quantitative purposes. In Chapter 2, I discussed the idea of "qualitative experiments" as a loosely structured way of collecting data by setting up a scenario and, basically, just seeing what happens. The focus is not on collecting quantifiable data but rather on witnessing interactions between people or things more holistically with the goal of inductively creating or understanding theory better.

In quantitative studies, data may be collected or "created" through **classic experimental design**. In the pursuit of valid and reliable results, the classic design entails much stricter procedures than qualitative designs. For reasons discussed below, classic designs are considered a more trustworthy way of collecting data for the purpose of statistical analysis than observational studies. As such, classic experimental design is the cornerstone of many scientific endeavors and is particularly associated with fields such as pharmacology for which only the highest standards of evidence are acceptable.

To understand the value of classic experimentation, it is necessary that I first discuss two major problems with drawing conclusions from data that were gathered observationally. These two problems concern omitted variable bias and simultaneity/reverse causality bias, which were first mentioned in Chapter 2.

Omitted variable bias occurs when a factor that is related to both the cause and outcome of a theorized causal relationship is left out of the analysis. For instance, during the 1970s, a series of studies linked coffee drinking to higher rates of cancer and heart disease. What the researchers failed to account for was the omitted variable "smoking," which was related to both higher coffee consumption and higher disease rates at the time. Once smoking was taken into account, the relationship between coffee drinking and disease rates disappeared, or even reversed itself, in subsequent studies.

The problem with observational studies is that, unless every conceivable omitted variable is taken into account, there is always the potential for bias. Something else can always be "lurking" below the radar, so to speak, and acting so as to confuse, or "confound," the cause-and-effect relationship being described. Classical experimentation overcomes this problem through the process of "random assignment," which is discussed below.

Another problem with drawing conclusions from observational data involves the possibility of **simultaneity/reverse causality bias**. Such relationships occur when variables are causally influencing one another, or when a theorized dependent variable is acting on an independent variable rather than vice versa. In such cases, the theorized influence of an independent variable on a dependent variable is either nonexistent or less than it seems. For instance, a social scientist might suggest that poor economic performance is systematically related to political instability. However, in a poorly designed project drawn from observational data, it might be uncertain whether or not political instability causes poor economic performance in whole or in part. The ability of a researcher to intervene in the data collection process translates into less chance for causal confusion, because the researcher is only observing effects subsequent to his or her introduction of different independent variables or treatments.

Classic experimentation involves three steps that help mitigate or overcome major problems associated with observational data collection. The first step involves random selection of subjects for a study. The second step entails dividing those subjects randomly into different groups. The third step involves the researcher introducing different values of an independent variable (a treatment or control) for each group (see Figure 4.7).

The first step, random selection, is important for classic experiments for the same reason that it is important for polling/survey research. Quantitative research seeks to understand trends within a population. If the results of an experiment are to apply to a wider population or the

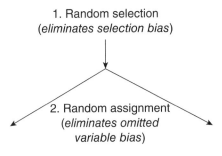

Figure 4.7:   The three steps of classic experimentation

opinions of a group to represent popular opinion, then random selection is central to the selection of a representative sample. In both cases, the larger the number of subjects, the more representative the sample. As the sample increases in size, the random characteristics of the sample, due to the law of large numbers, converge on the true characteristics of the overall population.

Unfortunately, in studies involving human beings, true random selection is impossible. Since no one can be made to participate in an experiment, random selection can only be approximated. In some cases, this might not be an enormous hurdle because the characteristics of those choosing to take part in a study might be unrelated to the phenomenon being studied. However, in other cases, such as psychological studies in which the desire to participate might have a strong correlation with other behavioral traits, caution must be taken in assessing the validity of experimental results.

Once a sample of subjects is selected, a researcher randomly divides the sample into different groups and assigns a different treatment (or no treatment, aka a control group) to each. Again, randomness is key. Dividing subjects randomly into treatment and control groups is the ONLY way to overcome the omitted variable problem that plagues purely observational research. In observational research, independent variables are confounded by other, lurking, variables that covary with both the independent variable in question and the outcome being investigated. This is because the behavior of one thing is often related to similar behaviors.

For instance, in an earlier example, I mentioned an observational study that drew the conclusion that coffee drinking was related to cancer rates. The problem was that, at the time of the study, smoking rates were related to both coffee drinking and cancer outcomes. Without including smoking as a control variable in the study, the relationship between coffee drinking and cancer rates were actually masking the true effect of smoking.

Now imagine a hypothetical experiment, rather than a simple observational study, that involves looking at the relationship between coffee drinking and cancer rates. If subjects were randomly assigned to two groups, one that would be asked to drink coffee while the other abstained, the confounding effects of smoking would become irrelevant because the distribution of smokers in both groups would be similar. As a matter of fact, there are potentially many personal habits that might be potentially associated with both coffee drinking and cancer rates that would be "averaged out" through this process and thus become irrelevant. Through random assignment, classic experiments eliminate all potential confounding variables at once. This is one of the main reasons classic experimentation can be considered the "gold standard" of data collection.

In addition to random selection and random assignment, classic experiments are characterized, as a third step, by the fact that it is the researcher, rather than the behavior of the subjects, that sets the value of the independent variables in the study. This too has important advantages over observational studies. First, since the researcher has more control over the environment, the values of independent variables are more likely to be measured more correctly and precisely. Second, since the researcher is causing changes in the values of the independent variable, he or she is more clearly responsible for changes in the dependent variable.

Thus, for the purposes of subsequent hypothesis testing, classic experiments yield better data than observational studies by eliminating or greatly mitigating problems associated with omitted variables, simultaneity/reverse causality, and measurement error. Classic experiments do not represent tests themselves, per se. However, they allow for the creation of data in a way that avoids the problems of quantitative data that have been collected and operationalized or observed more directly.

The biggest drawback of experimentation is that it is only feasible in certain cases. In many areas of human activity, it is either not possible or considered unethical to conduct experiments. An international relations scholar, for instance, cannot study the effects of nuclear weapons on country behavior by providing such weapons to some countries and withholding them from others. Likewise, an environmental scientist cannot pollute some areas and leave others unpolluted. In such cases, the use of observational data, with all its aforementioned drawbacks, is the only option for research.

Experiments may also be criticized in certain instances due to their restricted external validity. Since experiments often take place in specific, structured environments, the argument can be made that the data collected from such studies would not accurately reflect real-world conditions. In the social sciences, this is a particular problem as people often behave differently if they are in an "artificial" environment or know they are the subject of a scientific experiment (known as the **Hawthorne effect**).

One way to enhance external validity in the social sciences is to conduct **field experiments**. Field experiments utilize experimental methodologies "in the field"—that is to say, in real-world environments rather than in laboratories. Wantchekon (2003), for instance, oversaw an experiment in Benin that involved delivering different types of campaign messages to different villages to see how electoral behavior would be affected. In an example I mentioned earlier in the chapter, Gerber and Green (2000, 2008) have conducted field experiments across the United States involving differing forms of get-out-the-vote efforts (mail, telephone, face-to-face, "robocalls", etc.) to determine which methods are most effective.

Quasi- and Natural Experiments

It is often impossible to randomly assign subjects to different groups, particularly when dealing with human subjects. A **quasi-experiment** drops, for practical reasons, the experimental use of random assignment. In the coffee-drinking study mentioned above, it would be very difficult to rely on people to either drink certain amounts or abstain from coffee drinking as part of an experiment. A somewhat more realistic approach might be to divide self-reported coffee drinkers from noncoffee drinkers, offer both smoking cessation programs, and compare the resulting cancer rates. Like a classic experiment, the researcher is still controlling the value of the independent treatment, variable. However, absent random assignment, problems like potential omitted variable bias (e.g., other factors affecting cancer rates that could be related to coffee drinking) become an issue once more and can only be mitigated with statistical techniques.

The Swedish government conducted a quasi-experiment of sorts over a 13-year period from 1949 to 1961, when it added a school year in some school districts while keeping most districts the same. Lager, Jonas and Torssander's (2012) study of the effects of the different districts found that the added school year had a modest effect in reducing mortality among adults who had spent more time in school. While there was a clear difference in treatment between different school districts, the fact that they were chosen and assigned through political and bureaucratic processes meant that the investigational method is better described as a quasi-, rather than true classic experimentation.

A closely related way of collecting data is through the use of **natural experiments**. Natural experiments observe changes in the condition or behaviors of subjects that come about due to changes in their environment. In other words, the independent variable affecting subject behavior changes due to circumstances beyond the control of the actors and without the intervention of a researcher.

The question then becomes how the new circumstances affect outcomes. For instance, Glazer and Robbins (1985) analyze how the policy positions of congressional representatives change when the political views of their constituents change due to redistricting. In this case, redistricting serves a similar function to that of a researcher's treatment in classic experiment. However, absent random assignment, any attribution of a causal effect on political behavior due to redistricting is suspect due to the potential existence of other confounding variables.

Quasi- and natural experiments are comparatively stronger ways of collecting data for the purposes of empirical study than most other observational studies. However, absent the methodology of classic experiments, similar problems exist in attributing causal links between specific variables.

Conclusion

The procedures of model building, hypothesis creation, operationalization, measurement, and experimentation that I examine in this chapter all share a common purpose. Each measure is undertaken to set up the different types of tests of causal theory described in Chapter 5. They represent a bridge between theory and the assessment of how much empirical reality seems to accord to theoretical propositions. In Chapter 5, I present an overview of some of the common ways that hypotheses are assessed.

DISCUSSION QUESTIONS

4.1 Choose three potential independent variables that might be analyzed to help explain changes in the values of each of the dependent variables listed below:

Life expectancy

Weight gain or loss over a year

A student's final class grade

Poverty rates in a given city

4.2 Choose and justify what type of variable (continuous, discrete quantitative, categorical, or dichotomous) you would use to measure each type of variable:

Student major

Suicide rate

Number of prisons

Political party affiliation

Per capita income

Age

Car color

4.3 Write two hypotheses using the variables listed below. Identify the dependent and independent variables and the direction of the relationship.

Closeness of election results

Voter turnout

Total money contributed to the candidates

Number of political ads on television

4.4 Look at the following concepts:

Athleticism

Religiosity

Student motivation

Teaching effectiveness

For each one, think about how the concept could be measured empirically. Come up with an empirical measurable proxy variable for each. Next, break each concept down into two or more measurable concepts. Which approach seems more valid for the purposes of measurement?

4.5 What differentiates a hypothesis from a research question? Why is the distinction important?

4.6 Quasi-experiments are usually conducted because it is impossible or unethical to conduct a "classic experiment." Devise your own quasi-experiment and explain why a classic experiment was unfeasible.

5

Testing Hypotheses

Overview

This chapter presents a basic overview of some of the basic methods used to test quantitative hypotheses. It explains how researchers test hypotheses to see whether patterns exist linking the behavior of hypothesized independent to dependent variables. The primary discussion involves the use of inferential statistics in hypothesis testing, but it also looks at the role that nonstatistical "critical tests" play in confirming or disconfirming nonprobabilistic phenomena.

The chapter starts "from scratch" in discussing concepts like statistical significance before building up to a more sophisticated discussion of a variety of types of statistical tests that one encounters in scholarly research. The investigation of statistical methods uses **ordinary least squares (OLS)** regression as the jumping-off point for explaining many of the major statistical concepts. The chapter goes on to briefly discuss examples of common statistical tests, including everything from limited dependent variable tests like logit and probit to survival analysis and analysis of variance (**ANOVA**).

Introduction

To the uninitiated, statistical methods often represent the most daunting part of the social sciences. While qualitative studies are valuable and useful in a variety of contexts, it is impossible to understand large chunks of mainstream scholarship without acquiring a passing acquaintance with some of the main concepts involved in quantitative hypothesis testing. A recent analysis of leading sociological journals dating back to 1935, for instance, found that about two-thirds of the articles used some sort of quantitative methods (Hunter & Leahey, 2008). Another recent analysis of top political science and international relations journals found 57% to be quantitative in nature (Ruggeri et al., 2011). Even in fields many would associate with qualitative research such as nursing and anthropology, quantitative research is fairly common.

Quantitative, statistically oriented research is important in large part because it is used to understand whether or not trends in data exist that support theories and hypotheses. Whether testing hypotheses in sociology, politics, education, medicine, or almost any other field, statistical inferences help researchers verify that causal relationships exist in a more rigorous manner than evidence involving simple intuition, arguments, anecdotes, or trial and error.

In this chapter, I present an overview of some of the basic methods used to test quantitative hypotheses. The goal is to explain how researchers test hypotheses to see whether a pattern exists linking the behavior of hypothesized independent to dependent variables. I explore a variety of common types of statistical tests that one encounters in scholarly research. Where possible, I try to avoid dense technical discussion in favor of an admittedly somewhat breezier surface-level approach. Entire books cover many of the subjects in this chapter; my goal here is to help illuminate the basics rather than overwhelm with specifics. Before discussing the types of methods one tends to encounter in statistical analyses, however, it is useful to ask what it means to "test" hypotheses in the first place.

Hypothesis Testing and the Limits of Qualitative Research

Tests, as a general term, are conducted to determine whether something is likely to be true or not. It may be easiest to think of testing in a "descriptive" sense. Does the student know enough to answer the questions in the exam? Will an analysis of the blood sample reveal a disease? All tests, in fact, will yield answers that can be thought of as descriptive (i.e., answering simple factual questions) when considered in isolation. Hypotheses and testing can indeed be directed toward, and applied to, such factual questions. However, in the rest of this chapter, I discuss how hypotheses and associated tests can be used to evaluate causal propositions.

Hypothesis testing becomes associated with causality, rather than simple description, when linked to preexisting theories. Consider the example of a blood sample mentioned above. Simple blood work divorced from any preexisting theory might reveal differing levels of cholesterol, sugars, proteins, and other substances in the bloodstream. As a test of a causal hypothesis, however, a doctor would have met with a patient, developed an inductive theory of what might be ailing the patient, and utilized a targeted blood test to assess whether his or her suspicions were correct. This last type of testing that is utilized to see if something specific is true is the type of testing discussed in this chapter.

In this chapter, I discuss two types of hypothesis testing procedures associated with causal research. My primary focus is on statistical techniques that are ultimately grounded in **inferential statistics** that can help researchers decide if causality can be inferred from existing data. I also discuss the idea of **critical tests** that involve studying specific phenomenon to shed light on universal processes.

The terms *hypothesis* and *testing* are words we associate with the sciences—both natural and social. Scholars in the humanities would seldom claim to objectively "test" the types of relationships that they explore in their fields. On the other hand, hypothesis testing is considered so central to the natural sciences that it is easy to overlook the fact that much science also involves observation and theory building rather than hypothesis testing alone. In the social sciences, the terminology may sometimes lend itself to sloppy usage. Perhaps because terms like *hypothesis* sounds rigorous, scholars use them in contexts as misplaced as inductive, qualitative case study research.

To test a theory and its associated hypotheses, new data must be found for the purposes of testing. It would be tautological to assess the propositions of a theory by using evidence that was collected to build the theory in the first place—data that already support the argument being made. "Purely qualitative" research is by nature contextual, and data outside that context presumably do not exist.

The propositions of projects utilizing small-n "comparative methods" are not directly testable either. Comparative methodology allows for more convincing inductive theoretical argumentation because cases are selected so that potentially confounding factors (omitted variables) can be controlled to some degree and eliminated as likely alternate explanations. However, using comparative methods to deductively test theoretical propositions is problematic.

First, comparative case studies, while controlling for some major variables, also leave the door open for other alternate explanations. This is because in small-n research, it is difficult, and often impossible, to find cases that are either extremely similar (most similar) or extremely different (most different). Also, because small-n research requires having more observations than explanations,[1] it cannot usually control for a large number of potentially confounding variables in the same manner as large-n research. Coppedge (2002) describes the problem of "testing" at the small-n level, particularly for regional "comparativists," thus:

> Within-region comparison is often defended as a way of "controlling" for factors that the countries of the region have in common. [However] such "controls" would [only] be effective if there were zero variation on these factors. . . . The result is that many different explanations fit the available evidence; there is no way to rule some of them out, so they all seem to matter. In practice, how do scholars deal with this problem? Sometimes they interpret the evidence selectively, presenting the confirming evidence that they prefer for ideological or extraneous reasons. In the worst cases, they may even suppress disconfirming evidence, consciously or not. These practices amount to interpretations, not tests. (p. 11)

Another problem with treating small-n designs as tests is that the selection of cases in comparative projects is nonrandom. Recall from the earlier discussion of survey research in Chapter 2 that for predictions about a general population's characteristics to be valid, the sample that is chosen for study must be random. Without random selection, one cannot test whether a theoretical proposition is actually a general trend. While comparative projects can apply theoretical propositions to specific contextual cases (something that will be discussed in Chapter 6), general social trends cannot be confirmed or discounted without the tools of large-n testing.

Ragin (1987) advocates the use of Boolean algebra, a type of mathematics employing a series of dichotomous variables that function like on-off switches one might encounter in electrical engineering, to analyze small numbers of cases. While this approach and his subsequent introduction of "fuzzy sets" (Ragin, 2000), both of which represent recommended reading but are beyond the purvey of this work, add a certain rigor to small-n comparative analysis, the fundamental problem of small-n testing remains; namely, that absent the ability to control for large numbers of variables and absent random selection of cases, "tests" are bound to be misleading. Like any small-n analysis, Ragin's work is most useful in the

---

1. When more variables than cases exist, logical conclusions about causality cannot be drawn. This is known as "indeterminacy" and is sometimes referred to as the "many variables, small-n problem."

development of theories that can subsequently be tested using large-n statistical techniques.

Despite my misgivings about the uses of small-n research in hypothesis testing, there are uses of the comparative method in the type of applied "structured-focused" research that I will discuss in Chapter 6. A good example of this approach is used by Zangl (2008) when he evaluates institutionalist theories to examine differing outcomes of trade disputes between the United States and Europe under GATT (General Agreement on Tariffs and Trade) and the WTO (World Trade Organization). By holding most factors constant (primarily the actors and trade disputes involved), he can assess whether instituting more formal trade adjudication procedures is important in resolving trade disputes. However, Zangl studiously avoids the word "test" in his work (in favor of the more watered-down "evaluate") because he likely realizes that applying theories to a small number of cases can at best represent a "quasi-test" rather than the real deal.

Using small number of cases in these sorts of "quasi-tests" that add more evidence for a researcher's theory is generally most useful when (a) a causal phenomenon is more deterministic than probabilistic, (b) the basis of comparison are very similar cases, and (c) there are limited (if any) assertions of generality. First, "determinism" is important because probabilistic factors cannot be assessed in a small number of nonrandomly selected cases—only those factors that are necessary causes for every case. Second, the cases selected for comparison need to be very similar to avoid a variety of potential alternate causal factors. Practically speaking, this is most likely the case in a comparison of a single subject over multiple time periods. Last, the approach of "quasi-testing" is limited to those cases that are being evaluated. The implications of a theory can only be applied to the cases under examination rather than generalized to those outside of the purview of the study.

In short, researcher's should be careful to differentiate between small-n research that is used to build strong inductive arguments or is applied in a more "evaluative" context from research that is able to accurately test hypotheses in a general and probabilistic fashion. As Achen and Snidal (1989) put it, "Inferential rigor is not the best tool for what case studies should accomplish, and the comparative method works best when it enforces no such discipline," (p. 167) and comparativists should rather be guided by "common-sense rules of inference" rather than treating cases as if they were being subjected to strict testing procedures.

Ultimately, my goal is not to assert a narrow definition of a "test" by fiat but to help differentiate the process of hypothesis testing from other parts of the research process. A test is not something that is conducted concurrently with the process of theory building or data collection. It is also not to be confused with research designed to evaluate how causal mechanisms function in an applied context, as will be discussed in Chapter 6. Finally, testing is not the same as quantitative data collection, experimental data creation, or the operationalization of data discussed in Chapter 4, even if they are closely related.

Testing, as I use the term, is used to evaluate theories that suggest generalizable propositions, such as those found in midlevel and some macrolevel theories. The point of testing is to see whether things (beyond the context of the information used to develop a theory) occur with empirical regularity in a manner suggested by the theory. In testing whether "reality" accords with abstract theory, researchers mostly employ critical tests or utilize inferential statistics.

Hypothesis Testing Through Critical Tests

Many methodological discussions involve the use of statistics in testing hypotheses. The role of *critical tests* in hypothesis testing, however, often goes neglected. Critical tests involve the observation of a specific phenomenon to see whether the phenomenon confirms the findings of theories that predict universal phenomena. They are more frequently used in the natural, rather than social, sciences, where universal causality rarely, if ever, exists.

A classic example of a critical test from the natural sciences was Arthur Eddington's test of an aspect of Einstein's theory of general relativity that suggested that light waves should bend in the presence of gravity. Eddington devised a test of this theory by photographing a solar eclipse that occurred in 1919. His hypothesis suggested that if Einstein were correct, starlight from behind the sun should be observable in the middle of darkened sun. When his photographs revealed the presence of starlight within the eclipse, he could fairly surmise that Einstein's theory would have held up in the cases of any eclipse or, even more broadly, any interaction between light and gravity.

While statistical testing of hypotheses is designed with the expectation that "we will see this pattern of data" if a hypothesis is correct, using critical tests of hypotheses suggests that "we will see this thing" if a hypothesis is correct. A major difference between the two approaches is that statistics deal with probabilistic patterns, while critical tests deal with deterministic absolutes. In probabilistic studies, one example of something is never enough to confirm a trend. In studies of immutable phenomena, one example is all that is needed to prove or disprove what is happening universally.

Hypothesis Testing Through Statistical Analysis

Statistical analysis is the primary method of assessing data collected for the purpose of hypothesis testing. More specifically, hypothesis testing entails the use of different types of inferential statistics that establish the plausibility of theoretical propositions based on available data. As I will discuss, inferential statistics may be used to determine the likelihood that a nonrandom trend exists between the values of variables.

Statistical analyses are based on the information found in data sets. In Table 5.1, I provide an example of a small data set. Most data sets, whether contained in Microsoft Excel or a more sophisticated statistical program file, look roughly similar. Each observation (different patients in a study, different countries, etc.) is listed in the far left column. Different variable names are listed across the top row. To the right of each observation are the variable values associated with that observation.

Different sets of data have different characteristics depending on how and when the data were measured. **Longitudinal data** repeatedly measure a particular subject over time. For example, if a doctor was measuring the blood pressure of a particular patient repeatedly over time, the data would be considered longitudinal. **Cross-sectional data**, on the other

Table 5.1:   Example of a (Very Small) Data Set

Fruit	Color	Calories	Fat/g	Price	Sales
Apple	Red	100	0	1.99	15
Kiwi	Green	50	0.5	2.99	5
Banana	Yellow	105	0	0.99	25
Grapes	Green	105	0	2.99	20
Avocado	Green	275	27	3.99	5

hand, examine multiple subjects at a particular point in time. The "snap-shot" of the fruits in Table 1.1 would be an example of cross-sectional data. Last, when the two types of data are combined and multiple subjects are examined in multiple time periods, the data set can be said to be composed of **panel data**. Certain statistical tests require an understanding of what type of data are being analyzed.

Statistical Significance

In terms of hypothesis testing, the major goal of inferential data analysis is to determine the likelihood that a nonrandom pattern exists that would provide support for the hypotheses being tested. If data were randomly distributed, it would be clear that no pattern linking variables exists. The question then becomes, how do we know the difference between statistical trends and random data?

Take the example of a simple coin flip. What if we formed a hypothesis that a coin was a double-headed "trick" coin? If the coin were flipped once and landed on "heads," this would hardly provide strong evidence for our assertion. Why? Because half the time, the coin would land on heads through sheer random chance. The question is, How many times would we have to flip the coin until we were convinced that a nonrandom pattern existed?

There is no concrete answer to the question other than to say that the more times the coin lands on heads, the more convinced we would become that the result was nonrandom. A coin only lands on heads two times in a row one quarter, or 25% of the time; three times in a row, 12.50% of the time; four times, 6.25% of the time; and five times 3.125% of the time. At this point, there is a scientific convention that says if we witness a pattern in data that would only occur less than 5% of the time, we can "accept with confidence" the hypothesis that the coin is "fixed" (or reject the **null hypothesis** that suggests that the coin was not fixed). Of course, the 5% scientific convention is, simply that, a convention, and if the researcher wanted stronger evidence, he or she might, for instance, remain skeptical until the pattern reached 1% (7 heads in a row) or .1% probability (10 heads).

In the coin-flipping example, two factors increasingly convince an observer that the coin is "fixed." The first factor is the fact that the coin keeps landing on heads, while the second factor is how many times this happens. In statistics, the two factors that lend themselves to confirming or discounting a hypothesis are similarly the values that variables take and the number of observations that are available for testing.

Of course, flipping the coin and suggesting it always lands on heads is a simple example. What if the coin was flipped 50 times and ended up heads 30 times—Would this happen randomly more than 5% of the time? (Yes.) What about 40 times? (No.) What if we thought that the propensity of the coin to end up heads (the dependent variable) depended on the direction of the wind (an independent variable)? How big a difference would the resulting flips have to be for us to be convinced that wind direction was affecting the outcome?

Statistics suggest answers to such questions in probabilistic terms by ascertaining the **statistical significance** of the relationship between variables. Statistical significance indicates how likely it is that an expected or apparent pattern in the relationship between the values of two or more variables is, in fact, only a matter of random chance. Statistical significance is indicated by a p **value**, with p indicating the probability (expressed 0 through 1) of randomness. Thus a p value of .25 indicates that observed values would be likely to take such values 25% of the time through random chance alone. A result of $p < .05$ would indicate that between the values of two variables there is less than a 5% chance that the relationship indicated by the differing values of two variables is random.

Effect Size and Direction

If a relationship is found to be statistically significant at an acceptable level, a researcher then becomes interested in the magnitude, or **effect size**,[2] of the relationship. While statistical significance indicates how likely a relationship between variables exists, effect size indicates how much an independent variable is expected to influence a dependent variable.

A recent study (Mozaffarian, Hao, Rimm, Willett, & Hu, 2011) reported the effect size of diet on weight gain. The study statistically assessed the relationship of potato chips, sugar-sweetened beverages, and yogurt consumption (among other foods) on subject weight changes and found that all had a statistically significant effect. However, the effect sizes of the changes were quite different. There was a **positive relationship**, that is to say the values of consumption and weight tended in the same direction between potato chip consumption (1.69 pounds [lb] over 4-year periods) and sugary beverage consumption (about 1 lb). However, there was a

---

2. Effect size is also sometimes referred to as practical or clinical significance, terms that can be confusing because they can incorporate other factors that interpret the importance of effect size. Also, terminology-wise, *effect size* is easily distinguishable from statistical significance.

negative relationship between yogurt consumption and weight changes—with each additional serving of yogurt resulting in an expected loss of 0.82 lbs over the same period. In each example, the data revealed a statistically significant relationship, but the effect size and directions of the relationships differed considerably.

It should also be borne in mind that an analysis can yield a strong, statistically significant relationship between variables without displaying a large effect. The announcer for a recent commercial for diet pills repeatedly emphasized that the pills were proven to yield "statistically significant weight loss." While a strong statistical association is a good start, the commercial said nothing about how large the predicted weight loss would be—it could be 1 lb/kg or it could 10 times that—statistical significance says little by itself about the expected size of a relationship.

The concepts of statistical significance, effect size, and directionality are the cornerstones of hypothesis testing. The next section discusses the most common types of statistical operations used in data analysis, each of which, ultimately, seeks to establish at what level statistical significance exists and the size and direction of the relationship between independent and dependent variables.

Types of Statistical Tests

There are many, many types of statistical tests that are used to analyze data—enough to fill entire sections of libraries. However, there are a few basic types of common statistical operations with which every researcher should be familiar. Again, the goal is not to provide a comprehensive statistical education but rather provide a short overview of some of major statistical terms like OLS, ANOVA, logit, and probit that are very commonly encountered in mainstream scholarship.

Recall the previous chapter's discussion of how variables may be measured as continuous or discrete variables. Continuous variables include variables measured at both the interval and ratio levels. Discrete variables include categorical variables, which are measured ordinally or nominally, and "quantitative discrete variables," which only take on whole number values.

Other than the case of "quantitative discrete" (count-type, whole number) variables, variables are either continuous or categorical. The likely choice of most basic statistical operations depends on what types of variables the independent and dependent variables represent. There are four basic combinations of categorical and continuous variables when considering the independent and dependent variables: (1) either both are categorical, (2) both are continuous, (3) the dependent variable is categorical and the independent variable is categorical, or (4) the independent variable is categorical and the dependent variable is continuous. Quantitative discrete variables represent somewhat of an "in-between" case and are represented as such in Table 5.2, which displays some of the common statistical operations that are performed and how the choice of method depends on the combination of variable types being analyzed.

Table 5.2:   Analyses Commonly Used With Different Combinations of Variables

		Independent variable	
		Continuous	Categorical
Dependent variable	Continuous	*OLS regression*	*ANOVA* *difference of means* *(Poisson/negative binomial* If dependent variable is "quantitative discrete")
	Categorical	*Probit/logit regression*	*Cross-tabulation*

Notes. OLS regression, ordinary least squares regression; ANOVA, analysis of variance.

Regression Analysis

When one or more of the independent variables in a data set is continuous, it is typical to test hypotheses using **regression analysis**. As with other operations discussed in this chapter, there are many types of regression analysis. The purpose of all regression analysis is to determine what the expected value of a dependent variable is conditional on the values of one (bivariate regression) or more (multivariate regression) independent variables. To derive the expected value of the dependent variable, regression analysis calculates the average effect size and direction of the relationship with the independent variable(s) and determines whether that relationship is statistically significant.

In the following sections, I begin by discussing a particular type of regression model known as ordinary least squares, or OLS. I use the example of OLS to describe many of the fundamental statistical concepts that are found in a variety of regressions and statistical models. After my discussion of OLS, I describe several important issues encountered in regression analysis before moving on to a discussion of other types of commonly utilized statistical methods.

Ordinary Least Squares

Ordinary least squares, or OLS, regression was the first type of regression analysis developed[3] and is the most straightforward. The following discussion also allows for the introduction of most of the concepts necessary to understand the basics of other types of data analysis.

Below is an equation that describes a bivariate OLS regression.

Equation 5.1

$$y = \alpha + \beta x$$

This equation should look pretty familiar to anyone who paid attention during their high school math courses. It is the equation for a straight line, often expressed as $y = mx + b$, where the β represents the m, which is the slope ("rise over run") of the line, and α represents the b, or the y-intercept. y represents the value(s) taken by the dependent variable, and the x(s) represents the values taken by the independent variable (both of which the researcher has observed and/or quantified in advance).

The "α",[4] as I noted, is the y-intercept term. It's what the value of the dependent variable (y) would be if $x = 0$. This is useful information if we want to calculate the actual values of y from the values of x, but it does not say anything about how changes in x are expected to cause changes in y. Known as a **constant (or y-intercept)** the α term is something of a "statistical fix" that is necessary for predicting unknown outcomes after the β and x values are known, but it is not the value in which researchers are most interested.

---

3. The ordinary least squares approach to regression is most associated with Carl Gauss, who developed the approach in the years surrounding 1800.

4. α is also commonly denoted as β_0.

The value in which researchers are most interested is that of the β value. The β value is known as the **coefficient**, which mediates the relationship between the x's and the y's. In OLS regression, the meaning is very intuitive. The coefficient indicates how many units the dependent variable (y) is expected to change for each unit change in the independent variable.

For example, let's say that we know that $y = 10$, $x = 2$, and $\alpha = 2$. What is the coefficient? Plug the numbers in the above equation, do some simple algebra, and the coefficient emerges as $\beta = 4$. So, if $x = 3$, we would expect $y = 14$, and so on.

The value of β reflects the magnitude, or effect size, of the relationship between the independent and dependent variables. When it is larger, in either a positive or negative direction as indicated by its sign, the effect size of the relationship is greater. The simple example in the last paragraph showed how to derive a coefficient for particular values of two variables. OLS regression is used to derive a coefficient that indicates the expected effect size of the relationship between *all* the values taken by the independent (x) and dependent variables (y).

It would be easy to figure out β if there was a perfect relationship between the independent and dependent variables. For instance, if (disregarding a constant) different values of x were 2, 4, and 6 and the corresponding values of y were 4, 8, and 12, then the coefficient would equal 2 and a nice line with a slope = 2 could be drawn between the different data points as shown in Figure 5.1.

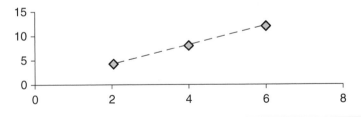

Figure 5.1: Simple linear relationship with a coefficient = 2

Unfortunately, in the real world, such exact relationships rarely exist between the independent and dependent variables. In addition to the values of the independent variable, random factors often influence the values of dependent variables. For example, let's say that we expect life expectancy (dependent variable) to be a function of the number of cigarettes (independent variable) a person smokes each day.

If the relationship were perfect, we might say that someone who does not smoke will live 85 years and that every cigarette consumed daily reduces that number by a year.

In the real world, while there is a relationship between life expectancy and smoking, it is far from a perfect relationship. Some people do not smoke, but they get hit by buses and die at a young age. On the other hand, some people, due to genetic good fortune or other factors, live to a ripe old age despite smoking. These other factors that change the value of the outcome from what would be expected are known as stochastic, or random, **error**.[5] An actual patterned set of data points from the real world would, rather than a straight line, more likely resemble something like Figure 5.2.

Due to real-world "error," it is necessary to add an additional term to the perfect linear relationship indicated in Equation 5.1 to account for the errors.

Equation 5.2

$$y = \alpha + \beta x + \varepsilon$$

The ε represents the "error term" and can be either positive or negative for any given set of values. For example, in the cigarette and life expectancy example, we observe someone smoking a dozen cigarettes a day and living only to age 40. The equation would be as follows:

$$40 = 85 + (-1)12 + (-33)$$

where 85 is the constant, 40 is the value of the dependent variable (life expectancy), –1 is our pretend coefficient, and 12 is the value of the independent variable (number of cigarettes). That leaves –33 as the error term, the difference from the expected pattern and the value of the dependent variable. Presumably, something "random" happened to the person that prevented him or her from living to his or her life expectancy.

---

5. "Error" and the term **residual** are related to each other. Errors are deviations from the expected "unseen" functional pattern that actually exists between variables in a population, while residuals are the actual deviations from the coefficient as calculated from the sample data. For simplicity's sake, I will stick with the more conceptual-minded term *error*, with the understanding that at times, the word residual may be more appropriate.

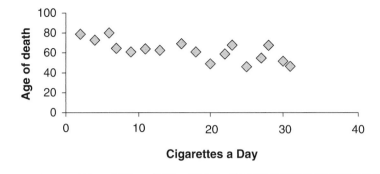

Figure 5.2:   Real-world data are not perfectly linear

In analyzing data, researchers derive the values of coefficients from the values of the errors, not the other way around. The value of a coefficient in a regression equation reflects the slope of a line that can be drawn such that the sum obtained by squaring all the errors and adding them up is minimized. By minimizing "squared" values, regression analysis weights larger errors less in calculating where the regression line belongs. A regression line with the slope of the coefficient is thus "fitted" to the data—slicing more or less down the middle of the data points as seen in Figure 5.3:

Determining the coefficient's value is only half the issue. As stated earlier, while it is important to derive the effect size of the coefficient, it is equally important to determine how "statistically significant" the coefficient is. It is important to know not only how "big" the relationship is but also how "strong." Just because a coefficient appears big does

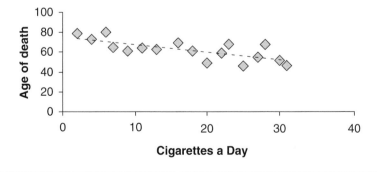

Figure 5.3:   A sample regression line

not mean a pattern exists at all. For instance, look at Figure 5.4. It appears that a positive pattern exists, but how sure can we know that the values of the x and y variables are not only related by random chance? It's not something that can be easily "eyeballed."

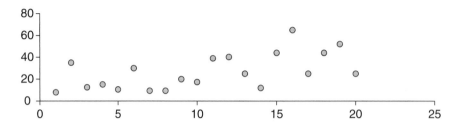

Figure 5.4:   Is there a statistically significant relationship here?

Statistical significance indicates the probability that the pattern of values observed for the independent and dependent variables is only coincidental. If we accept $p = .05$ as a relationship that is "statistically significant," then we are 95% confident that the relationship between the variables is not random. There still remains, of course, a 5% chance that on accepting that the relationship exists, a researcher is nevertheless committing a "Type I error"—which is a fancy way of saying a "false positive."[6]

There are three primary factors of interest in determining the statistical significance of a coefficient:

1. The effect size of the coefficient

2. The amount of error in the data

3. The number of observations being analyzed

In an OLS regression, a *t* **test** is calculated using these three considerations. The *t* value of an OLS coefficient indicates the ratio of "signal" to "noise" by dividing a coefficient's value (the effect size) by the "standard error" of the regression.

---

6. While a Type I error indicates that a researcher is led to believe that a relationship exists that is actually a product of random chance, a Type II error, or false negative, is the opposite. In these cases, a researcher misses a pattern that exists, believing instead that a relationship between variables is only random.

Equation 5.3

$$t\,\text{value} = \frac{\beta}{SE} = \frac{\beta}{\sqrt{\dfrac{SSR}{n-k-1}}}$$

Where β is the coefficient, SSR is the sum of squared residuals, or total error (the "white noise"), n is the number of observations, and k is the number of variables. It is not as important to memorize the above formula as it is to understand the intuition behind it.

The *standard error* of the estimated coefficient simply involves taking the square root of the ratio of the total amount of error (or SSR) to the number of observations (minus "degrees of freedom"). The last point about the number of observations is crucial: Because it is in the denominator, more observations reduce the **standard error of the estimate**. This means that as more data are collected, statistical patterns emerge more clearly as the "white noise" of error subsides. In turn, as observations increase and the standard error becomes smaller, the t value becomes larger for a given coefficient β.

After the t value is calculated, it is converted to a p value using a t distribution, which indicates the probability of a particular t value occurring in the same way that drawing a bell curve of people's heights could be used to determine the probability that someone was over or under a certain measurement. There is thus an inverse relationship between t values and p values. As t values increase, p values decrease. Neither the t nor p values are affected by the direction of the association between the variables.

If the preceding paragraphs seemed overwhelming, the main points to remember are simply that a t value will increase and a p value decrease, when, all other things being equal,

- a coefficient becomes "larger" (in a positive or negative direction),
- the amount of error decreases, or
- the number of observations increases.

When any of these conditions are met, it becomes clearer that a nonrandom pattern exists between independent and dependent variables, the relationship is more likely to be significant, and a researcher's hypothesis more likely to be accepted. Most other tests of statistical significance that are not t tests employ similar calculations that incorporate effect size, error, and the number of observations.

In illustrating the above concepts, I have used simple examples of OLS regressions employing only two variables, an independent and dependent variable. Comparatively few studies only employ bivariate regression, however. Most utilize multivariate regression, which allows a researcher to analyze how multiple independent variables affect a dependent variable. The same basic concepts that apply to simple bivariate regression also apply to multivariate regression. Multivariate regression, however, allows a researcher to engage in the process of statistically **controlling** each independent variable.

If we examine a multivariate OLS equation, it looks the same as the bivariate version except that additional coefficients and independent variables (x) are introduced where the numbered subscripts indicate different independent variables.

Equation 5.4

$$y = \alpha + \beta x_1 + \beta x_2 + \beta x_3 + \cdots + \beta x_n + \varepsilon$$

The nice thing about multivariate regression is that the independent influence of each variable can be derived while controlling for the values of every other variable in the equation. This is important because most trends are caused by numerous factors that might be related to one another.

For instance, climatologists often consider the factors that influence global climate change. The dependent variable in a climatological model might be an aggregate measurement of global temperatures. The most obvious independent variables might include different types of greenhouse gases such as carbon dioxide and methane. What about other factors that influence climate change and might be correlated with greenhouse gas emissions and global temperatures? If a researcher does not control for factors such as changes in solar radiation, volcanic activity, and other climatological cycles in his or her analysis, the coefficients derived from simply analyzing the relationship of greenhouse gases to climate change might produce biased coefficients.

If a researcher wants to understand the independent effects of each, he or she needs to add the extra variables to the analysis. The coefficients that are subsequently calculated will show the independent effect of greenhouse gases by controlling, or holding steady, the values of the other variables, as well as the independent effects of those other variables. Multivariate analysis thus allows a researcher to analyze each variable **ceterus parabus**, all things being equal, in respect to the other variables in the equation (see Figure 5.5).

A problem arises, however, if any variable that would be correlated to the outcome *and* another independent variable is left out of the equation. This results in **omitted variable bias**, and the values derived for the remaining coefficients will be biased because they will reflect, in part, the influence of the variable that has been left out just as the analysis of asbestos factory workers would have exaggerated the effect of exposure to asbestos if a researcher did not control for cigarette smoking.

Many types of regression, like OLS, are susceptible to charges of omitted variable bias, because analyses are built on quantitative observational data rather than experimental data. As was discussed in Chapter 4, classic experiments overcome the problem of omitted variables through random assignment. Regression analyses based on nonexperimental data must, therefore, include every possible independent variable (x) that is related to the outcome (y) and at least one of the independent variables if it is to be considered unbiased.

Avoiding omitted variable bias is just one of the hurdles to overcome if the results of a regression analysis are to be viewed as unbiased. The next section describes some of the other conditions required for the common regression models employed in quantitative research.

Heteroscedasticity and Other Big Words

The basic mathematical operations underlying basic OLS regression require several conditions to be met if the analysis is to yield valid results. These conditions are known as the Gaussian or **Gauss–Markov**

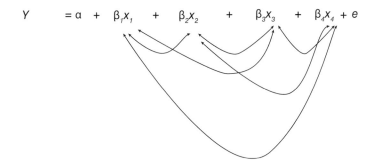

Each of these variables is analyzed while
controlling for the other variables

Figure 5.5:   Control and ceteris paribus

assumptions. One assumption demands that the error terms in the data being considered need to be distributed in a truly random manner; that is, they cannot be related to the independent variable, and if you add up the total error, it will equal zero. This should be the case (or close to the ideal case) when no omitted variables exist and many observations exist.

Another assumption is that the variance of the error terms has to be consistent throughout the set of observations for a variable. In other words, some data points might be plotted more precisely, with less chance of error, or random factors, affecting them than others. If this is the case, then the data are characterized by **heteroscedasticity** (a mouthful of a word that means "different dispersion" in Greek, depicted in Figure 5.6.) and are not suitable for the basic regression because they result in biased standard errors, thus increasing the potential for "false-positive results." Like other problems, however, there are statistical "fixes" that have been developed to overcome this problem in more sophisticated analyses.

Another potential pitfall involves data that are *autocorrelated*. For a regression to accurately estimate standard errors, the error terms, again, have to be truly random in nature. **Autocorrelation** results when the errors are related to each other over space or time. This is a particular problem with longitudinal data, when characteristics of the same subjects are observed over repeated periods of time. The problem is that each present observation is correlated with earlier observations which are, in turn, correlated with outcomes. Thus, past outcomes act as omitted variables that bias the coefficients derived from analyzing present independent variables.

For instance, if a study on blood pressure medication was being conducted, the strongest influence on a particular subject's blood pressure at a given time might not be the subject's dietary, exercise, or medicinal habits but, rather, what the subject's blood pressure had been the last time it

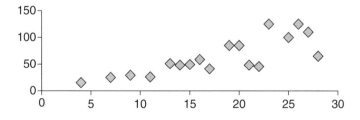

Figure 5.6:   Heteroscedasticity

was checked. If a researcher wants to understand what present factors influence a patient's blood pressure, he or she needs to take measures to filter out the influence of the past on present outcomes.

Fortunately, measures can be taken to deal with autocorrelation as well. Once it has been determined to exist ("Durbin–Watson" tests are common for this), the solution is sometimes as simple as including past variables' values as their own variable in a regression to control for the influence of the past. As with heteroscedasticity, failing to account for autocorrelation will bias standard errors in a way that generally makes it more likely that false-positive results will occur.

Another major issue that must be borne in mind when working with multivariate regression involves the issues of **collinearity** or **multicollinearity.** Perfect collinearity results when the values of an independent variable are perfectly predictable as a (linear) function of one or more of the other variables. If, for example, the value of a variable must equal 1 when the values of the other variables are 0, then a perfectly multicollinear relationship exists.

When perfect (multi)collinearity exists, a regression analysis cannot be conducted. To explain why, think about the earlier example of controlling for factors such as solar radiation in analyzing global climate change. If solar radiation were perfectly correlated with carbon dioxide levels, for instance, a researcher would be unable to statistically derive a coefficient for either factor because it would be unclear what variable was influencing global temperatures.

A common figure used to illustrate the concept of collinearity is that of a Venn diagram, as shown in Figure 5.7. The two large circles represent the observations of independent variables. The more highly correlated the variables are, the larger the area of "overlap" depicted in the diagram, and the more useful data that are "eaten up" that would aid in the regression analysis.

In terms of the climate change example, Douglass, Clader, Christy, Michaels, and Belsley (2003) analyze whether or not collinearity between El Niño climate cycles and volcanic activity that appeared during a similar period in time might affect estimates of the independent effects of either, thus masking their true influence on global temperatures. After conducting their analysis, the authors found that, while correlated to a certain degree, the degree of correlation and associated collinearity were not serious enough to change the conclusions of earlier authors.

Two main things can be done to mitigate collinearity. If two variables are highly correlated with one another in the first place, it is best to either

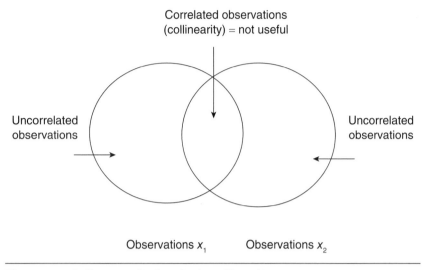

Correlated observations
(collinearity) = not useful

Uncorrelated
observations

Uncorrelated
observations

Observations x_1 Observations x_2

Figure 5.7:   Collinearity displayed using a Venn diagram

choose the best (most theoretically appropriate) one or, when that cannot be determined, use different regressions for each variable. The other solution to collinearity is simply to collect more data. Generally speaking, more data are always better when it comes to large-n analysis. This is particularly true when high levels of collinearity exist, because more data are needed to compensate for the data that are "lost."

A final issue with regression analysis involves the potential for **simultaneity/reverse causality bias**. This concept has been discussed in earlier chapters; it means that an independent variable is influenced by a dependent variable in whole or in part. In economics, the relationship between supply and demand is an example of this phenomenon. If a researcher attempts to estimate the effect of one on another, he or she has to account for the fact that each influences the other at the same time.

If the relationship modeled in a regression equation is not one in which the causality flows exclusively from the independent to the dependent variable, then the coefficients that are obtained for independent variables will be inflated. This is due to the fact that effects of the dependent variable are subsumed into the coefficient(s) of one or more independent variables just as if it were an omitted variable. A true unbiased coefficient β will be calculated and reported as β + the amount of influence of the dependent variable. If causality is completely reversed and an independent variable does not affect a dependent variable but is actually affected by the dependent variable, the true coefficient of the relationship would be 0. However, the coefficient would "look normal," because its value would equal β, which is really 0, plus the dependent variable's influence. The mathematics of regression analysis do not discriminate based on the directionality of the relationship, but the interpretation of coefficients as representative of the effect of x on y will be incorrect.

Dealing with simultaneity/reverse causality can be difficult. Sometimes a researcher can simply argue the implausibility of a dependent variable influencing a dependent variable. For instance, it is clear that smoking makes people sick, while getting sick rarely makes people pick up smoking. Other times a researcher can choose independent variables whose values reflect data that temporally preceded the data indicated by the dependent variable.[7]

In a recent paper, Piff, Stancato, Côté, Mendoza-Denton, and Keltner (2012) report the findings of seven quasi-experiments (mainly involving observing traffic violations and people cheating at games) that revealed a significant link between unethical behavior and higher socioeconomic status. The research design of the authors does not entirely make clear whether unethical behavior leads to wealth or wealth leads to unethical behavior. Although the authors make a fairly convincing argument for the latter, the presence of correlation is clearer than the causal direction of the relationship.

Regression With "Limited Dependent Variables"

Thus far, I have illustrated the main concepts of statistical inference through the use of OLS regression analysis. OLS regression is only used, however, when a dependent variable takes on continuous variables. However, when the dependent variable is not continuous, many of the Gauss–Markov assumptions concerning the nature of the error terms would be violated if OLS regression were used. Consider the simple graph in Figure 5.8, which displays how the values of observations would be plotted if the dependent variable took on only two values (dichotomous).

---

7. Another, sophisticated method of dealing with causality bias is through the use of "instrumental variables." An extended discussion of such variables is beyond the purview of this book. In short, however, researchers might find a variable that is related to a causally questionable independent variable (but not to other variables in a model) and indirectly "substitute" the new variable for the old variable.

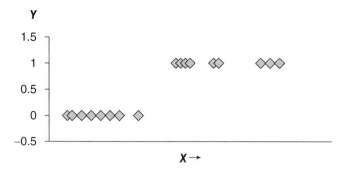

Figure 5.8:   How a dichotomous dependent variable would look (with a continuous independent "x" variable)

Common sense itself would seem to dictate that fitting a line to the data would be inappropriate. More to the point, however, a line would indicate that predicted values existed for the dependent value that lay in-between the only two values that the dependent variable may take. Since the nature of the data is such that decimals do not exist, these predicted values are meaningless. The same would be true for any plot involving a discrete dependent variable, no matter how many values it took.

Therefore, another subset of regressions is used when the dependent variable is "limited," that is, it takes on only certain, usually binary or discrete (quantitative or categorical) values. The type of independent variables being analyzed is generally not important, except that other types of statistical operations tend to be preferable when all of the independent variables are categorical.

Fortunately, the same concepts and issues involved in OLS regression are also central to other types of regression. The goal is still to determine the size and direction of coefficients and the level of their statistical significance. The same assumptions concerning heteroscedasticity, autocorrelation, collinearity, and simultaneity/reverse causality also apply.

When the dependent variable being analyzed is "limited," researchers use different methods to conduct their regressions. Without getting too in depth, regression with limited dependent variables involves transforming the output of a linear regression through various "links" that yield different predictive outputs. Below I look at a few of the common types of regression that are used when values taken by the dependent variable are not continuous.

Logit

Perhaps the most intuitive of these types of regressions is **logit regression**. The simplest type of logit, binomial logit, is used when a dependent variable is dichotomous. While the formulas for logit analysis take several forms, depending on the needs of the researcher, the one that lends itself to the most interpretable form is as follows:

Equation 5.5

$$\text{prob}(y = 1) = \frac{1}{1 + e^{-(\alpha + \beta_1 x_1 + \beta_2 x_2 + \cdots + \beta_n x_n + \varepsilon)}}$$

I place this formula here as a point of illustration rather than memorization. A couple of points about the equation bear mentioning. First, the output of the equation no longer indicates simply the expected value of "y" as a unit. Rather, logit models determine the expected *probability*, expressed 0 through 1, of a particular dependent variable value equaling 1 (assuming the dichotomous variable takes the traditional values of 1 or 0) given the values of the independent variables. Since a researcher is dealing with only two potential outcomes, the expression of probabilities, rather than units, makes sense.

The other point is that, once obtained, the coefficient/effect size is impossible for most people to interpret just by looking at its value.[8] As the equation indicates, the β coefficients that are calculated no longer indicate the "slope" of a line in which y changes a certain amount of units for every unit change in x. They still mediate the relationship between x and y but only as transformed through a complex mathematical transformation.

So, how then, do we make sense out of a logit output? The most common way of doing so entails keeping all the values of the x variables constant, with the exception of one, and then "plugging in" alternate values of the variable to see how the probability of y occurring changes as the values of the chosen variable change. This can be thought of as **baseline analysis**, because all variables, except one, are set at a baseline so that the effects of a particular variable may be examined.

For example, a common dichotomous dependent variable that has been used in the field of international relations indicates whether two

---

8. The direction of the relationship, however, would still be indicated by the sign of the coefficient.

countries engage in armed conflict during a given year or not (conflict, no conflict). If a researcher ran a regression testing the hypotheses that levels of trade and joint-democracy (whether both countries are democratic or not) and whether or not one of the countries had nuclear weapons were the likely determinants of peace or conflict, he or she would derive a set of coefficients and associated standard errors that was associated with each variable.

The researcher could, one at a time, then investigate the predicted effect of each coefficient. For example, if he or she wanted to understand the effects of trade, the researcher could establish a "baseline" of zero for the other two variables (effectively eliminating them from the equation) and then simply plug in two different values for trade into the logit model (Equation 5.5) after the appropriate coefficients have been calculated. The different probabilities of the y value resulting from the different x values would provide a substantive idea of the effect of trade on conflict. In Table 5.3, we see that, based on the coefficients obtained from a logit regression, increasing trade between countries from 0 to 12 million U.S. dollars would be expected to lower their conflict risk from 5% to 4%.

The following is a quick rundown of other types of commonly used regressions when the dependent variable is limited (not continuous as with OLS).

Probit

Very similar to logit regression, **probit regression** is also most commonly used when the dependent variable is dichotomous. The two types of regression yield almost exactly the same coefficients given the same data. Before the age of computers, logit regression was actually

Table 5.3:   Sample Baseline Analysis: Change in Conflict Likelihood

All variables equal zero or their average value	Baseline Probability = 5% (All Variables Equal Zero or Their Average Value)	
	New Probability (%)	Change (%)
Trade = 12 million U.S. dollars	3	−2
Joint-democracy = 1	2	−3
Nuclear weapons = 1	1	−4

developed, in part, as a computationally less demanding way to derive the same information as a probit analysis. Only in very unusual cases involving large numbers of expected probabilities near 0 or 1 will the estimates for these two methods diverge. The two methods are largely considered interchangeable and a matter of "researcher preference."

Ordered Logit and Probit

Simply an extension of the logit and probit models, **ordered logit and probit regressions** are often used when a dependent variable is ordinal (and takes more than two values) in nature. Instead of assessing the probability that a dichotomous dependent variable equals 1, these types of regression assess the probability that the dependent variable takes each of the values within the range of values taken by the ordinal variable given the values of the independent variables.

Poisson and Negative Binomial Regression

While logit- and probit-type regressions are commonly associated with categorical dependent variables that are either dichotomous or take a small number of ordinal values, **Poisson** and **negative binomial regressions** are used when the dependent variable is "quantitative discrete." Such quantitative discrete variables generally describe the number of times something happened, or, an "event count."

As was discussed in Chapter 4, some types of variables take only whole numbers (or integers) and are, therefore, not continuous. Just as a woman can't be half pregnant or have 2.5 children, neither can there be fractions of votes in Congress, assassination attempts on heads of state, or asteroid strikes against the earth's surface. When the dependent variable represents such "event counts," OLS regression is not sufficient.

A good example of the difference between the use of logit and Poisson analyses can be found in Crichlow (2002). In examining the link between legislator personalities and voting behavior, Crichlow uses a logit analysis in determining that a pattern existed between legislator personality traits and likelihood to vote for a *particular piece of trade legislation* (the Helms–Burton Act). However, in determining whether a pattern existed between legislator personality and the *number of votes* legislators cast for free trade legislation overall, he conducts a Poisson regression.

Negative binomial regression is actually a subset of Poisson regression and is also known as "gamma-Poisson." It tends to be used more frequently, because the assumptions underlying the variability of the data being analyzed are less strict than is the case with a Poisson regression. In either case, however, the analysis of event count variables will be more valid than would be the case were OLS (incorrectly) employed.

Survival Models

Survival models represent special types of regression that are used when a researcher wants to see the effect that independent variables have on the probability that a certain event will happen over a given period of time. The dependent value generally indicates, for each observation, the presence or absence of some type of failure or "mortality," either literally such as in medical studies, or figuratively, such as in a study of students dropping out of high school. Cioffi-Revilla (1983), for instance, uses survival model analysis to understand the factors determining the length of time Italian governments tended to survive before collapsing.

The most common type of survival models are "proportional hazard models," the best known of which is the **Cox regression model**. Cox analysis involves a calculation to determine a "baseline hazard function" (which determines how "failure rates" vary over time), which can then be interacted with calculated variable coefficients to determine a **hazard ratio**.

A variable's hazard ratio suggests how, if a variable value were to increase one unit, the likelihood of "failure" would increase or decrease. If the hazard ratio is determined to be 1, then the variable is having no effect. If the hazard ratio is determined to be 2, then an increase in one unit of a variable would be expected to double the chance of failure/mortality (**ceterus parabus**). If the hazard ratio is .5, then a unit increase would be expected to reduce the chance of mortality by 50%. How big a hazard ratio is required for a coefficient to be considered statistically significant is, as always, a matter of measuring the size of the effect compared with sample variability and sample size.

Cross-Tabulation Analysis

When a researcher wants to test hypotheses that solely involve categorical variables (nominal or ordinal), he or she often begins by constructing a cross-tabulation, or **contingency table**. While statistical analyses in these situations can be conducted through the "limited dependent variable" regressions discussed earlier, cross-tabulations are often preferred as a more "intuitive" way of examining categorical variables.

A cross-tabulation table simply involves creating a matrix that displays the possible values of one variable on the x-axis, the values taken by the other variable on the y-axis,[9] and the joint frequency of each variable in each cell. Table 5.4 shows a simple example.

As is the case in our other analyses, the first thing we want to know involves statistical significance. Are the frequencies displayed likely to be a result of random chance or are they due to some nonrandom association between the variables? At the same time, we want to know something about the strength, or effect size of the relationship.

The most common test of statistical significance is known as **chi-square testing**. Chi-square testing simply involves obtaining a chi-square value that is a function of the frequencies that are witnessed and the "expected" frequencies if the relationship were truly random. The p value is then obtained from the chi-square value by comparing it to a chi-square distribution.

If there is a statistically significant relationship between the variables, then a researcher might desire to know something about the strength of the relationship. An intuitive way to assess effect size in these instances is to ask the question How much better can we predict the value taken by a variable given the information provided by another variable?

A researcher may answer this question by calculating a statistic that indicates the **proportional reduction of error**, or PRE. Using the example of Table 5.4, we can calculate one such PRE statistic known as Goodman and Kruskal's lambda (λ).

Looking at the total number of (imaginary) voters on Table 5.4, we can see that more voters prefer the Democrat Party (30) over the Republican Party (20). If you were to guess individually which party each voter supports, the best guess, absent other information, would to be to guess that each voter supports the Democrats (because the odds are in your favor for each guess). The probability you would be right each time would be .60 (60%), and the probability you would be wrong would be .40 (40%).

However, if you knew what region each person was from you would guess differently. Every time you guessed the political party of someone

---

9. The interpretation of cross-tabulation analysis is not sensitive to simultaneity/reverse causation bias in the same way as regression analysis. Thus, while the specification of an independent and dependent variable might be important theoretically, it is not so mathematically.

Table 5.4:   Simple Contingency Table/Cross-Tabulation

Political Party Preference

	Republican	Democrat	Total
North	5	20	25
South	15	10	25
Total	20	30	

from the South, you would guess Republican, and every time you knew someone was from the North, you would guess Democrat. In this case, you would be right 15 out of 25 times among southerners (probability = .60) and wrong 10 out of 25 times (.40). Among northerners, you would be right 20 out of 25 times (.80) and wrong 5 out of 25 times (.20). In total, you would be right 35 out of 50 times (.70), given the additional information provided by region and the probability of being wrong would be .30.

How much did the probability of being wrong decline given the information added by the "region" variable? The lambda statistic is calculated by subtracting the number of errors with the new information from the number of errors without that information and then dividing by the original number of errors to obtain a percentage, or proportion, of the original probability. Thus

$$PRE = \frac{\text{Original error probability} - \text{New error probability}}{\text{Original error probability}} = \frac{.40 - .30}{.40} = .25$$

While lambda is one of the most intuitive PRE statistics, it is only applicable when the variables under analysis are nominal. Other PRE measures are used when (at least) one of the variables takes on ordinal values. Goodman–Kruskal's Gamma, Tau-a, Tau-b, and Tau-c are all examples of ways to assess the effect size of the relationship between variables in a cross-tabulation. The choice of which measurement is used depends on factors such as the total number of observations and the number of potential values taken by each of the variables.

Cross-tabulation analysis is most associated with bivariate analysis. However, control variables may be introduced as well. Table 5.5 displays how a contingency table would appear when a control variable is introduced.

In theory, control variables could be introduced indefinitely into the analysis. However, because a major advantage of cross-tabulation analysis involves its "intuitiveness" in simpler situations, a researcher would likely choose to conduct a regression analysis as the control variables start to add up.

Difference-of-Means Tests and ANOVA

The statistical procedures I have discussed thus far—regression analysis and cross-tabulation—are mostly associated with the study of observational data. In contrast, **difference-of-means tests**, and particularly ANOVA-type tests, are often used to analyze experimental data. The reason is simple. Difference-of-means tests and ANOVA are generally used when independent variables are categorical and dependent variables are continuous. The independent variable in classic experiments is categorical and nominal in nature and takes values such as control, Treatment 1, Treatment 2, etc. The effect, or outcome of each trial in an experiment, however, is most commonly a continuous variable. For example, a

Table 5.5: Contingency Table/Cross-Tabulation Controlling for Income

		Political Party Preference		
		Republican	Democrat	Total
North	High Income	3	7	10
	Low Income	2	13	15
South	High Income	10	4	14
	Low Income	5	6	11
	Total	20	30	

dependent variable in an experiment might indicate the blood pressure of a subject taking either a medication or a placebo.

Difference-of-means tests, also known simply as t tests (or "Student's t"), are very straightforward and easy to interpret.[10] They are used when the independent variable takes only two values. Thus, observations fall either into one group or another. The question being analyzed is whether the values of the dependent variable associated with one group are different enough from the values of the other group to be considered statistically significant. Here again, statistical significance is calculated as a function of both the observed values and the number of observations in the samples. The effect size of the difference is also very intuitive. It's simply the difference in the means of the two groups.

The t test is something that I mentioned earlier in regard to regression analysis. In the case of regression, the two "groups" are the effect size of the coefficient as it is calculated through regression analysis and the "null hypothesis" of the coefficient being zero. The math is exactly the same when comparing regression coefficients as it is with any two groups being analyzed side by side.

As with other statistical operations, there are several types of difference-of-means/t tests, the choice of which depends on factors such as the variance and size of the samples. Difference-of-means tests, in general, are intuitive and flexible in that they may be used when the samples are of different sizes or when they are small (under 30 observations). The major downside, however, is that they can only be used when there are two groups (i.e., the independent variable takes only two values).

ANOVA cannot be used for small samples, but it can be used when the independent variable takes multiple values. ANOVA stands for "analysis of variance" and, like many other statistical operations, analyzes data based on factors involving the "spread" and number of observed variable values.

With ANOVA, the researcher is assessing whether the values of the dependent variables in each group (each different value of a categorical independent variable) are different enough from one another for those differences to be considered statistically significant. To assess statistical

---

10. Regression analysis can be used in similar situations as a difference-of-means test when the independent variable is dichotomous and the dependent variable is continuous. However, since the "magnitude" of a difference-of-means test is simply the difference in the means of the two groups, it is generally regarded as more intuitive than a regression analysis would be.

significance, an **F test** is employed. An F test calculates a p value based on the ratio of the variance between categories to variance of the observations within each category. Intuitively, this means that an F test is essentially a signal-to-noise statistic like other tests used to assess significance.

In terms of effect size, ANOVA relies on a statistic known as **Eta-squared**. Eta-squared reveals how much of the variance of the values of the dependent variable are a result of variance in the independent variables. It can be interpreted in the same way as an **r-squared (r^2) value** (the square of the correlation coefficient between two variables). If, for instance, the eta-square of an ANOVA were .56, then 56% of the variances of the dependent variable can be explained by variation in the independent variables.

The most common type of ANOVA is known as one-way ANOVA and is sufficient for the analysis of the output of many classical experiments. Like the t tests, there are also different variations on ANOVA that rely on assumptions different from one another. Analysis of covariance (ANCOVA), for instance, is flexible enough to incorporate multiple independent variables that are both continuous and categorical. Multivariate analysis of variance (MANOVA) analyzes cases when there are multiple dependent variables. The choice of method often reflects the structure of the experiment from which the data being analyzed are derived, with more sophisticated experimental designs relying on more sophisticated statistical designs to interpret the results.

What Does It Look Like?

Thus far, I have discussed concepts like variables, coefficients, standard error, and statistical significance. For the uninitiated, all these undoubtedly seem a bit overwhelming. However, once these concepts are intuitively mastered, the results of most quantitative analyses become accessible and understandable. Most results, when presented, have roughly similar formats providing information about the major statistical concepts I have discussed.

Tables 5.6 and 5.7 are "typical" tables showing the results of an OLS regression analysis. Table 5.6 shows what types of information are typically displayed, while Table 5.7 fills in the blanks with pretend illustrative data. In each table, a title, which usually mentions the dependent variable by name, is provided at the top. On the left-hand side are the independent variables. On the top row are the different models that are tested. While sometimes only one model is tested, sometimes researchers might test alternative models alongside one another. This is done for a variety of reasons, including when two variables might be collinear (in Table 5.7, e.g., "milk" and "chocolate milk" might be collinear and thus better tested in different models) or to show that any statistical associations are **robust** under different model conditions.

Within each cell of the table are numbers that usually reveal something about the effect size and error of the relationship between the independent variable on the left and the dependent variable. In the OLS example (Table 5.7), these numbers usually represent coefficient sizes and standard errors. Other types of statistical outputs might have other types of calculations here such as "hazard ratios" found in survival analysis. Often associated with each cell are asterisks that indicate whether or not a relationship is considered statistically significant and, if so, at what level. I often tell students that "if nothing else, just look for the asterisks" because they will reveal the most important associations uncovered by a researcher.

Each model will also have additional information that tells how many observations were analyzed in each model and the **goodness-of-fit statistic**

Table 5.6:   Elements Making Up (Most) Regression Output Tables

	Title: Type of Analysis Indicating What Affects the Dependent Variable		
	Model 1	*Model 2*	*Model 3*
Independent variable	Coefficient (standard error or something similar)*	Coefficient (standard error or something similar)***	Coefficient (standard error or something similar)
Independent variable	Coefficient (standard error or something similar)**	Coefficient (standard error or something similar)	Coefficient (standard error or something similar)*
Independent variable	Coefficient (standard error or something similar)	Coefficient (standard error or something similar)*	Coefficient (standard error or something similar)
n	Number of observations	Number of observations	Number of observations
Goodness-of-fit statistic	R^2, pseudo-r^2, log likelihood, etc.	R^2, pseudo-r^2, log likelihood, etc.	R^2, pseudo-r^2, log likelihood, etc.

*$p < .10$; **$p < .05$; ***$p < .01$.

Table 5.7:   Sample Regression Output[a]

	Title: OLS analysis of factors affecting student weight gain (kg/year)		
	Model 1	Model 2	Model 3
Pizza	1.05 (.51)*	1.15 (.27)***	0.75 (.43)
Tacos	0.33 (.12)**	0.45 (.41)	0.45 (.22)*
Milk	−0.12 (.49)	−0.15 (.07)*	
Chocolate milk	0.08 (.13)		0.25 (.33)
n	105	105	105
r^2	0.31	0.29	0.24

Note. OLS, ordinary least squares.

a. Made up data.

$*p < .05; **p < .01; ***p < .001.$

for each model. The observations are simply noted by the letter n. Goodness-of-fit statistics take many forms depending on the type of statistical model used. OLS models use an r^2 *statistic,* which as I first described in Chapter 2, indicates how much of the total spread, or variance, of data points in a model can be associated with movements in the values of all the independent variables. Other common statistics that might describe models in terms of their total "fit" include chi-square statistics and "pseudo" r^2 tests. These statistics are all used to assess the total explanatory power of one model compared with another.

Data Dredging and Hypothesis Testing

Oftentimes, researchers have an incentive to obtain statistically significant results when testing hypotheses. Such results often lend themselves to publish-ability in the academic world and marketability in the business and medical worlds. *Data dredging,* also known as data fishing or snooping, entails a purposeful search for statistically significant relationships that are obtained by "playing with the numbers" until a false-positive relationship is uncovered.

Data dredging takes advantage of the fact that statistical patterns are probabilistic and that there is always the chance for false-positive ("Type 1") results. Using the convention that a hypothesis is confirmed when $p < .05$, there can still be up to a 1 in 20 chance that any given relationship between an independent and dependent variable simply occurred through random chance. A researcher seeking a statistically significant result can simply choose to test and retest different sets of variables or different sets of data until that result is obtained by random chance.

Data dredging can be seen as the misuse of the practice of *data mining*.[11] Data mining, in general, entails using computers to conduct large-scale statistical analysis of data sets in the search for correlative patterns of data. The practice of data mining can, in many instances, be a very useful way of uncovering trends that form the bases for theoretical conclusions. As such, data mining is a consummately inductive process of research.

Data dredging, however, perverts the process of data mining by using "pattern searching" as a deductive tool in hypothesis verification. I stated earlier the importance of using data for the purposes of testing a theory different from those that are used for building a theory. The use of data dredging essentially means that the same data used to find a statistical trend are being rereferenced as evidence that a more general trend exists.

The difference between data dredging and the more positive uses of data mining point to the importance of being able to holistically frame the process of research in our minds. While generally not intentional, qualitative researchers who invent hypotheses and then claim to have "proven" their hypotheses by applying them to their inductive research are engaged in a similar methodological debacle as those intentionally setting out to dredge data. Understanding the distinctions between research meant to build theories and generate hypotheses versus research used to test, evaluate, and apply theoretical propositions is central to a sound understanding of research methodology.

Conclusion

This chapter served as an overview of the most essential features of data analysis techniques used across the social and natural sciences. The overview I've provided in this chapter is sufficient for an understanding of most books and articles that constitute scholarship in a variety of fields.

For those new to inferential statistics in particular, the information I have discussed is a solid, but not sufficient, start for researchers wanting

---

11. Data dredging was once referred to simply as "data mining." As the positive applications of data mining have become widespread, the term *data dredging* has become a term used to describe the dark side of data mining practices.

to conduct their own quantitative research. There are simply too many considerations that go into "valid" data analysis to cover in the course of one chapter. For a more in-depth discussion of the particular methods I have mentioned, there are hundreds of books and websites that can provide more detailed descriptions.

Fortunately, however, there are a few, simple concepts that tie together almost all statistical research. The main point of all the statistical operations discussed in this chapter is to determine the likelihood that, when controlling for other important variables, a nonrandom pattern exists that ties together the independent variables with the dependent variables in a study. After statistical significance is established, the question becomes how large the effect of one variable on another is expected to be (effect size) and the direction of the effect. Finally, the type of statistical test depends in large part on the types of variables being analyzed.

Many research projects, of course, do not involve quantitative data analysis. Only certain types of research and research questions are amenable to this type of hypothesis testing and verification. Types of research that cannot be tested statistically include microlevel research that deals with particular situations and perceptions as well as some types of macrolevel theory, especially those that are structural in nature.

This does not mean, however, that there is no way to assess theories that are not amenable to quantitative testing. The last part of the research process involves the use of "applied theory"—putting a theory into action and observing how it helps a researcher understand the "real world," while, in turn, the "real world" aids in understanding the strengths and shortcomings of a particular theory. I now turn to the purposes and methods used in theoretical application.

DISCUSSION QUESTIONS

5.1 An example in Chapter 5 mentions a radio advertisement for a weight-loss product that repeatedly boasted that the product had been shown to produce "statistically significant" weight loss. Why might a customer nevertheless be dissatisfied with the product's role in helping him or her lose weight?

5.2 What type of regression analysis (OLS, logit/probit, negative binomial/Poisson) would you use to analyze the following quantitative hypotheses (*hint:* how would you characterize the dependent variables)?

   a. The worse a country's economy gets, the more likely its leader will be defeated at the next election.

   b. The higher the unemployment rate becomes, the higher the crime rate becomes.

   c. The more hours you study, the more top grades you will receive.

5.3 Given the following variables, what type of analysis would you likely use to analyze their quantitative relationship (cross-tabulation, difference-of-means testing [e.g., a t test, ANOVA, or OLS]). Why?

Independent variable (IV): Present or absence of death penalty laws in 20 different countries

Dependent variable (DV): National murder rates

   IV: Whether participants in a large medical study were given a treatment A, treatment B, or placebo in a medical trial
   DV: Blood pressure rates
   IV: Whether a country has parliamentary or presidential system
   DV: Whether a country has a unicameral or bicameral legislature
   IV: The level of humidity each day last year
   DV: The level of rainfall each evening last year

5.4 Take a look at the following output from a (made up) regression analysis:

OLS Regression of Level of Student Educational Satisfaction at a University

Average class size	−5.53 (2.21)*
Instructor ratings	10.23 (2.42)**
Number of extracurricular activities	−2.21 (3.54)
National ranking of schools	−.02 (1.35)
n	125
r^2	.23

Notes. OLS, ordinary least squares. Standard errors in parentheses.
*$p < .05$; **$p < .01$.

What are the dependent and independent variables? What appear to be the strongest associations between variables? What do the signs mean before the significant coefficients? What do the n and the r^2 indicate?

PART IV

Using Theory

6

Applying Theory and Evaluating the "Real World"

Overview

This chapter discusses several aspects of theoretical application and how it dovetails with both qualitative and quantitative research. It discusses the nature of case study research in general and how the study of particular events can serve different purposes depending on the goal of the research. It argues that understanding the relation between theory and case is essential in interpreting or conducting research. The chapter also explores how theories can help "predict the future" by framing assumptions and forming the basis of models and simulations designed to help understand future events.

The chapter concludes with a discussion of more "informal" trial-and-error–type approaches to applying and revising theory. It looks at how businesses and institutions evolve knowledge through incremental **trial-and-error approaches** and why this is sometimes a suboptimal approach to learning new information. Finally, the chapter concludes with a discussion of the cyclical nature of research and how the continual refinement of theoretical knowledge will continue to be the goal of collective research efforts.

Introduction

Roger Smith (2002) once wrote that he did "not believe that 'knowledge' and 'science' have 'sakes'" (p. 199). For Smith, research in the social sciences, in particular, should serve the ultimate goal of bettering society rather than merely satiating the curiosity of a handful of ivory-tower academics.

Although in this author's opinion there is room for "pure science" and the spirit of exploration, most research is ultimately intended to yield practical applications or further our ability to interpret real-world situations. While much of the big picture of research involves the development and testing of theory, once a researcher has deemed a theory credible, it can often be applied in an effort to solve real-world problems and better understand social and natural events. Even what is often termed *basic science* in the natural sciences, that is to say the pursuit of knowledge in areas without any discernible immediate applications, is usually thought of as the groundwork for potential future innovation.

A researcher in many fields, such as physics and economics, explicitly differentiates "applied" branches from those that focus more on theory building or experimentation and testing. Whether labeled as such or not, applied researchers in many fields rely on theoreticians to provide the groundwork for their research, while making the work of theoreticians more useful and meaningful.

Applied researchers focus their efforts on what I describe as the final steps of the research process (even if, as I describe later, research can be described as cyclical and, in a sense, never ending). By **applied theory/ applied theoretical research**, I mean any endeavor that utilizes preexisting theories and understandings as the framework for problem solving while also contributing feedback as to whether or not such theories adequately address "real-world" issues or require further refinement.

Oftentimes, we do not necessarily think of practitioners in applied vocations as conducting "research." Individual doctors and nurses, for example, might view themselves exclusively as practitioners rather than researchers. While it is true that research is not the primary goal of most medical professionals, and while most do not contribute to journals or write books, both individual doctors and nurses, as well as the community of medical professionals as a whole, provide feedback over time about practices that seem to work or not work. Some might consider it stretching the definition of "research" a bit, but there are many who contribute to the evolution of knowledge in applied fields in individually small but collectively large ways.

Beyond allowing researchers to understand more about the present, applied research also allows researchers to make predictions about the future. One of the most common questions students ask me is whether they can write a paper about whether this or that will likely happen. My answer is always the same: While we cannot directly "research" things that have not occurred, we can use well-supported preexisting theories about what has happened in the past to deduce possible outcomes in the future. The use of theory in providing a framework for predictions and simulations of future outcomes is an important application of research in many fields.

In this chapter, I discuss several aspects of theoretical application. First, I discuss the nature of case study research in general and how the study of particular events can serve different purposes depending on the goal of the research. Second, I look at the method of "structured-focused analysis," and how theory is used to interpret events in the social sciences and the humanities. Third, I examine how simulations serve as predictive tools that help social and natural scientists determine the ramifications of their theory for future events.

I wrap up the chapter with a discussion of more "informal" trial-and-error–type approaches to applying and revising theory. Many theories, including all purely qualitative theories, are not assessed through quantitative data collection and large-n testing. Such theories, however, can be simply put into action to see if they work as theorized and then be revised and reevaluated as necessary. I'll discuss the advantages and disadvantages of this evolutionary approach to knowledge and how "best practices" may or may not emerge as a result.

The Varied Nature of "Case Study" Research

While the end of the chapter discusses the application of theory in professional environments, I begin with a discussion of how theory is applied in the "scholarly" world. While the two are not entirely distinct, scholars often deal with subject matters from a distance that does not exist in more hands-on environments. **Case study research** often involves an outside-in look[1] at events or processes to understand better what is happening and (often) why it is happening.

For a seemingly simple concept, however, there is a lot of debate over what a case study actually is and why it is useful for research. To offer a couple of well-thought-out definitions, Gerring (2004) describes a case study as "the intensive study of a single unit for the purpose of understanding a larger class of (similar) units" (p. 342), while George and Bennett (2005) suggest that it is "the subset of qualitative methods that aspires to cumulative and progressive generalizations about social life

---

1. If the researcher directly observes the events of a case study, he or she will generally attempt to "take a step back" analytically to make sense of what has happened.

and seeks to develop and apply clear standards for judging whether some generalizations fit the social world better than others" (p. 19).

Both quotations suggest that a case study is generally thought of as part of a larger class of phenomena rather than something that occurs in isolation. Both definitions taken together also suggest that there is more than one role played by case study in relation to theory. Gerring's (2004) definition focuses more on the role of case studies in building theory while noting the role cases can have in "judging whether some generalizations fit the social world." George and Bennett (2005) see an applied, evaluative role for case studies.

The framework I suggest for understanding case studies[2] divides the objectives into two main groups. From the onset of a project, a researcher should recognize whether his or her case study project is being undertaken because (1) the researcher is more interested in the theoretical ramifications of the case study or (2) the researcher is more interested in understanding the real-world case itself. In reality, many case studies combine both goals, but it remains essential for a researcher to recognize the different purposes he or she is pursuing in his or her investigation.

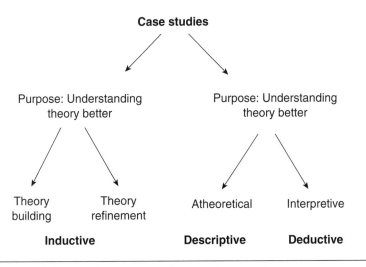

Figure 6.1:   Breakdown of the purposes of case study research

---

2. The framework I suggest is a somewhat reworked version of the discussion of case studies by Lijphart (1971, pp. 691–693).

Case Study Purpose Number 1: Understanding Theory Better

If one thinks of theory as central to a case study project, then building or reevaluating theory in light of the findings of that case study is a primary goal. Many research projects involving inductive theory building are conducted through case study research. In some cases, case studies are context dependent and purely "idiographic" in nature. Other times, case studies help researchers understand causal relationships that can be (tentatively) used to construct broader-based theories.

Case studies are also used to evaluate preexisting theories and help determine where improvements can be made. Some (Eckstein, 1975, p. 127; Flyvbjerg, 2006) have suggested that certain case studies can be used as a sort of "test" of hypotheses. If a theory suggests that a particular phenomenon is universal in nature, and a case study researcher observes an event that contradicts the theory's predictions, then the original theory's universalistic claim can be said to be falsified. As Karl Popper famously explained, if a hypothesis suggests that all swans are white and a black swan is discovered, then the original theory has been discredited.

Case studies that establish or discredit universal claims are known as **critical (or "crucial") case studies**. The term *critical case study* is similar to the idea of critical testing that I described in Chapter 6. While the term *critical test* suggests a purposeful, hands-on attempt by a researcher to create a situation for the purposes of hypothesis testing, case study research might be thought of as more observationally oriented.

Critical tests and cases lend themselves more to the natural sciences than the social sciences. Social scientists mostly study events that are context dependent or represent probabilistic, but not universalistic, trends. For probabilistic trends, case studies cannot represent "tests" because they are composed of a limited, nonrandom sample of related phenomena. As such, there is no way to determine if a particular case is a typical case or one that defies the norm.

In these instances, even though case study research does not provide a definitive test of a theory, a researcher can still evaluate what elements of the real-world case seem to accord with a theory and what things do not. When the observations within a case study do not seem to fit what a theory would suggest, then a researcher seeks to understand whether extenuating circumstances (previously unconsidered variables, unforeseen variable interactions, etc.) define the case as unusual or whether the assumptions of a theory are credible. Revising theories to account for outlying cases is part of the process as well.

Thinking of the research process as a whole, there are two points at which theoretical revision through case study research is common. The first point is when a theory is first inductively derived. In the initial phases of research, the process of theory building and revision tends to go hand in hand (the cyclical nature of qualitative research depicted by the two-way arrow at the beginning of the model). As theory is constructed, it begins to guide and shape the further collection of data, which in turn shapes theory and so on.

The second area in which theoretical reevaluation takes place is toward the "end" of the research process. Using a theory that has already been posited, a researcher looks at an original case study (not one used to build the theory) and evaluates the causal processes suggested by the theory in light of the new case. The research process, of course, never really ends, and the lessons learned from these case studies form the basis for newer, improved theories that may be used in the future.

Case Study Purpose Number 2: Understanding a Case Better

Thinking back to the original point that most research is not simply for "knowledge's sake," case studies represent not only an exercise in theory building and development, but also an opportunity to interpret events through a theoretical lens. Case studies in which events, rather than theory, are the central focus of analysis can either be atheoretical/descriptive or theoretical/causal in focus. These are, again, ideal types, and many case studies will combine both goals.

If a case study is primarily or solely descriptive, then the purpose is to relay events to an audience without causal speculation. Stories written by objective-minded journalists would fit this category, as would many primary-type sources. Historians, archaeologists, and anthropologists often focus on detailed, "thick"ly descriptive accounts of newly discovered factual information.

Many researchers would like to know, however, why and how events occur as they do. Application of theoretical research to the understanding of events might not be a standard part of the "scientific method," but it is an essential difference between the rigorous analysis that characterizes scholarly thought and traditional learning. In our everyday lives, we constantly make judgments about causality based on heuristic "mental shortcuts" gleaned from earlier experiences and beliefs. Such judgments are inherently biased, however, and different conclusions would be drawn by different people under the same circumstances. Applying theory in research allows a researcher to employ a well-defined set of causal propositions, which have been derived through earlier research or deduction, to rigorously assess, point by point, what is transpiring in a real-world case. When the focus of research is on applying theoretical lessons, researchers can also use the framework of theory to draw conclusions about what might happen in the future if the theories' predictions are correct.

The next section describes "structured-focused" analysis, which is used by researchers for both the "theory-centered" and "case-centered" type of case study research that has been described above.

Structured-Focused Analysis/Interpretative Case Study Research[3]

Structured-focused analysis represents a way of evaluating small-n case study research through the lens of previously derived theories. As George and Bennett (2005) write,

> The method of structured, focused comparison is simple and straightforward. The method is "structured" in that each researcher writes general questions that reflect the research objective and that these questions are asked of each case under study to guide and standardize data collection. . . . It is "focused" in that it only deals with certain aspects of the historical cases involved. (p. 67)

The research questions mentioned by George and Bennett are questions that reflect aspects of the theory that is being used to understand the case study. These "questions" are not the same as the straightforward and falsifiable hypothetical statements that guide large-n data testing, but rather more general theoretical propositions to better understand how causality works in a particular case. Oftentimes, cases are analyzed by using multiple theoretical frameworks that help explain different aspects of an event.

The use of the word "focused" is meant to distinguish this type of analysis from holistic exploratory or descriptive research surrounding

---

3. There is no standardized terminology for the use of single cases in applied research that I am describing. I use the term structured-focused analysis, but, as I mention in this section, this term has, up until now, been reserved for comparative research. The term "structured focused" also has the downside that it is rarely used outside of political science. The term "interpretative case study" also indicates the deductive-type goals of case studies that I am discussing but might also be confused with the type of inductive, interpretivist research I describe in Chapter 2.

a certain event. Rather than a more passive focus on the case itself, structured-focused analysis seeks to balance theoretical understanding with theoretical application. With theory anchoring the research, researchers want to focus on aspects of the case that are specifically related to the theory at hand. For instance, a case study about German-Russian relations on the brink of the First World War could encompass a huge number of factors, from the structure of their governments to colonial histories to the personalities of the leaders involved. However, a structured-focused analysis focusing on Robert Jervis's "spiral model," which suggests that measures enhancing military preparedness create mutual suspicion and increases the prospects for war, would reign in the myriad explanations for the conflict and concentrate on one particular aspect.

The term *structured focused* is generally coupled with the term *comparison*, indicating that the methodological framework is generally applied to comparative case study projects. There is no reason, however, that the same method cannot be applied to a single case study. The basic structured-focused approach does not really change based on the number of cases analyzed. A feminist scholar could, for example, research just Saudi Arabia through the lens of theories related to gender stratification, or he or she could apply such theories to multiple countries.

Part of the reason structured-focus research is flexible in its case selection is because it differs in approach and goals from the traditional "comparative methods" like most similar case design. The differences illustrate the importance of the holistic understanding of research methodology suggested in the research model (Figure 1.1). The comparative method is most associated with building convincing theories of causality through carefully designed case selection. Only when theories built through comparative methods are applied to other cases does the method converge with structured-focused analysis.

Rather than theory building, structured-focused analysis is primarily concerned with theory application and reevaluation. Unlike with the comparative method, researchers employing structured-focused analysis are not starting "from scratch"—a preexisting body of work already exists that may be drawn on as a source of inquiry. The focus is not on building a theory as much as it is on understanding the world through the "lens" of that theory while, at the same time, reconsidering potential shortcomings of the theory when reality diverges from expectations.

Due to the "applied" focus of structured-focused analysis versus the "theory-building" focus of the comparative method, case selection does not need to be, in a sense, as rigorous in structured-focused comparison as it does in "most similar" and other comparative designs. With structured-focused analysis, the theoretical focus of analysis is "prebuilt," and the analysis begins as a deductive exercise built on theoretical assumptions and variables. To reach this point, however, the stricter case selection of **comparative methodologies** might have been used earlier in the research process to eliminate alternate theories and build the sound foundation on which the original theory was built.

The coupling of comparative methodologies with structured-focused comparison is a particularly effective strategy for exclusively qualitative researchers. The powerful inductive logic of the comparative method can be used to build strong theories. Those same theories, once constructed, can be applied and reevaluated by selecting other cases for analysis.

Another use of structured-focused analysis is as a complement to both earlier theory-building and large-n quantitative analysis. As with any qualitative research, the advantage of structured-focused analysis is that an analysis is centered on causality. While quantitative testing can lend credibility to the propositions of a causal theory, assessing empirical data patterns is not a direct test of causality itself. As a matter of fact, there is usually no way to directly "test" causal mechanisms in quantitative research because they tend to be "invisible" to the researcher.

Structured-focused analysis allows researcher to improve on purely large-n analysis in two ways. First, by examining events as they have actually occurred, a researcher might find evidence suggesting that causal conclusions drawn from the large-n analysis are misleading.

Several examples concerning how a structured-focused analysis can help evaluate the findings of a quantitative study are discussed by Sambanis (2004) in his discussion of a comparative, structured-focused study of numerous countries and the reasons they did or did not seem to conform to the findings of an earlier quantitative study conducted by Collier and Hoeffler (2002).

Sambanis (2004) discusses, for example, how the Collier–Hoeffler model found that reliance on primary commodities like oil was statistically associated with civil war outbreaks due to theorized factors such as the ability of groups to fund themselves through the export of such commodities. On closer examination through case study research, however, examples of countries like Azerbaijan, an oil rich country that fought a civil war in the early 1990s, were found to fit the statistical pattern but not the causal story. In the example of Azerbaijan, oil fields were located far from the area of conflict and could not have conceivably influenced the outbreak of conflict in the manner theorized. Other types of issues uncovered by the structured-focused analysis included potentially misleading operationalization of variable values in particular cases, the presence of potentially omitted variables, and poor conceptual fits between what variables were supposed to measure and what they actually did. All of these findings laid the groundwork for better, more refined, analyses in the future, and none of them could have been understood without the closer examination provided by structured-focused analysis.

Structured-focused analysis also helps a researcher understand why some cases do not conform to the expectations of a probabilistic large-n analysis. Since large-n analyses only examine behavioral trends, they often have little to say about outlying cases that deviate from the patterns of data that have been uncovered. Structured-focused analysis involves the examination of particular cases and the way in which variables relate to each other in those particular circumstances. Reasons for outlying behavior can be learned by studying what other factors might have influenced the outcomes of events such that they did not conform to expectations.

The downside of interpreting case studies through the lens of theory, however, is captured by Dobson (1999), who cautions that theory is "a way or seeing and not seeing" (p. 261). Bad research of this type will result in the same biased conclusions that occur when researchers set off to "prove a hypothesis." The goal of such research is not to show that a case "works" a certain way theoretically but, rather, to keep in mind that few cases accord perfectly with theory and to understand the gaps in our theoretical understandings.

When a researcher conducts structured-focused analysis, he or she learns about both the cases being studied as well as the theories used to study them. This "two-way street," between theory and application, in which each informs the other, is a key to understanding small-n research in the applied context. In this sense, applied research mirrors inductive theory building, except that it begins as a deductive investigation that is guided by theory rather than an attempt to build a novel theory from scratch.

Simulations

Simulations use models to determine what would happen under different situations using data that are "made up." Simulation research entails inputting different data values into a model and observing the outcome.

The models themselves have already been derived from earlier theoretical research and testing. Simulations are "run" by introducing data into a preexisting model framework and determining what one could expect to happen if the original model is correct.

Simulations often help researchers understand the implications of their models under conditions when preexisting data are not readily available for analysis. Oftentimes, this means using simulations to "predict the future" based on models derived from current data. Forecasting future trends involves relying on models and understandings based on information that has been based on past events.

There is a phrase in computer science, however, "garbage in, garbage out," which captures the potential downside of simulation research. Simulation research is only as valid as the model and data on which it is built. If either the parameters of the original model or the data used in a simulation are incorrect, then the results of the simulation will be misleading.

Nowhere is the use of simulations more controversial than those used in long-term climatological models, particularly those related to global climate change. Based on the study of past data, climatologists have developed models and algorithms that help them understand global weather patterns and temperatures. Using the parameters of models created from historical climatological data, climatologists attempt to simulate how, given further assumptions about factors like greenhouse gas output, cloud and ice cover, and solar behavior, temperatures will change the world globally and regionally.

Critics, of course, point out that the parameters explaining past climate behavior, even if largely correct, might not adequately explain future climate behavior due to changing conditions. Furthermore, assumptions about future data such as greenhouse gas emissions can vary widely. While a simulation can make a range of predictions based on alternate values of the input variables involved, there is no way to conclusively argue for particular values of future empirical data. While past data and modeling seem to indicate that human-made global change is likely to occur, the predicted effects of such warming vary widely given varied assumptions about future climate conditions and the models used to understand their effect.

Simulation research, however, need not be based on large amounts of quantitative data like that used in climatology. Sometimes simulations take the form of one-shot trials that are meant to approximate reality. For instance, there is a theory that the moon was created when a Mars-sized object struck the earth a "glancing blow" billions of years ago. A scientist, making assumptions about the relative size, speed, and density of the two objects might attempt to replicate the collision on a much smaller scale by firing one object at another in a laboratory and extrapolating, from the results, whether the results were suggestive of the real event. These types of simulations are similar to critical tests, except that they rest on a variety of assumptions concerning how well the parameters of the test truly approximate reality.

Simulation research is an interesting way of applying theory in an effort to determine how, if the assumptions of the theory are correct, reality might unfold. The more complicated and tentative the assumptions involved in constructing a simulation, however, the more questionable simulation outputs become. If future data suggest, however, that a simulation was indeed correct in its predictions, then the underlying model becomes an increasingly useful and powerful tool for further research.

Theory Into Action: Praxis and Best Practices

The ultimate application of theory involves a researcher actually putting theory into action in the real world. Sometimes theory is transformed into real-world applications after extensive quantitative study and/or experimentation. Such is the case when governments introduce new environmental legislation or pharmaceutical companies bring a new drug to market.

Many times, however, the road from theory to practice is more direct. For example, qualitative theories are not amenable to quantitative testing. Even with certain theories that might be amenable to empirical testing, the data gathering and analysis necessary for quantitative analysis might be difficult or deemed inappropriate. In such cases, researchers often take preexisting theories and simply put them into action and observe the results.

One useful term associated with "real-world" learning is **cybernetics**, which is derived from the Greek word for "steering." Research into cybernetics examines information feedback loops in a variety of settings involving both machines and people. When studying the behavior of people in settings such as businesses and bureaucracies, cybernetics assumes people act somewhat like thermostats who continually adjust their behavior based on information about their environment (Glasersfeld, 2000, p. 95).

Another term associated with a theory-into-action approach to learning is the word **praxis**. Associated originally with Aristotle, the term has been used in slightly different ways by philosophers including Immanuel Kant and Karl Marx. Today, the term is also well-known as the name for a series of tests required of American teachers seeking professional certification.

I use the term *praxis* here to describe the cyclical process through which theories are applied to the real world, which, in turn, provides experience that allows for **theoretical refinement**. The process of praxis is embedded into the qualitative grounded theory that I discussed briefly in Chapter 1. Praxis, however, can generally be thought of as a less formal approach that does not generally involve the categorization and codification associated with grounded research.

Another term that is largely synonymous with praxis is **action research**. In describing the centrality of such research to education doctoral work, Zambo (2011) summarizes how her students proceed with such action research:

> They select a problem to solve at their worksite, explain why it is a challenge of importance to them, investigate the literature for viable solutions, take action, collect and analyze data to determine the effectiveness of their action, reflect on what they learned, and consider their next steps. (p. 264)

Another good example of a research field that relies heavily on the methodology of praxis and cybernetic learning is nursing research. Since nursing is "hands-on" by nature, it makes sense that much scholarly research is developed by those who have spent time "in the trenches" reflecting on what practices are effective and what are not. There is a large body of nursing theory that is taught to nursing students so that they may apply the "best practices" that have been compiled over the years.

The concept of "best practices" applies to other areas as well. While the idea of best practices may simply seem like a corporate buzzword, it does describe well the pursuit of optimal outcomes through a process of evolutionary, trial-and-error–type research. While the "research" of the business and public sectors may not be as formal as that associated with the scholar or the scientist in a lab coat, accumulated field experience that is passed down in either oral or written form is attempting to answer a basic research question: What factors are most likely to account for desirable outcomes?

The trial-and-error, informal "best practices"–driven praxis approach to knowledge is almost certainly the most common way research, in the broad sense, is conducted in professional and bureaucratic settings around the world. Such approaches, however, are not always the optimal way of approaching knowledge. Lindblom (1959) described processes of bureaucratic change and learning in terms of their "incrementalism." Organizational change rarely occurs quickly and most "muddle through" in a search for more rational and efficient ways of doing business.

Praxis-type research improves on theory through a process of incremental evolution. The problem with this type of research, as with the process of evolution in the natural world, is that sometimes things get "off track." Evolutionary dead ends and extinctions are the norm in the natural world, not the exception. In the world of research, evolutionary approaches can lead to the development of "bad practices" when things like habit, personality, and institutional inertia substitute for objectivity and rationality. It is hard to escape from the bad practices that develop because they become the starting point for future learning. Under such circumstances, only someone who takes a step back and looks at the big picture can effectively right the sinking ship. Management and human resource consultants make a living trying to rationalize governmental and business practices that have taken such evolutionary wrong turns and led to the institutionalization of faulty conclusions and suboptimal practices.

Research as a Cyclical Process

The thrust of this chapter has been to describe how the process of applying theory represents the final culmination of the research process. The ability to use what we have learned is the most important reason to pursue knowledge in the first place.

The process of causal research, however, can rarely be said to have come to an end. There are few theories that perfectly predict reality, need no modification, or cannot be built on in the search for newer and more comprehensive theories. As I have discussed throughout this chapter, the process of theoretical application often goes hand in hand with the process of theory reinterpretation and revision.

Since research as a whole is cyclical and unending, it is, by nature, a collaborative effort. Some researchers build theories, others find ways to test those theories, and yet others find ways to apply those theories. Researchers continually draw on one another's work and build on lessons learned by others to create new and more interesting theories and to learn from the shortcomings of the past.

Conclusion

In this relatively brief final chapter, I discussed how researchers go about using theory to help solve "real-world" problems, understand past events, or even make predictions about the future. There are multiple paths to reaching the "applied" stage of research and multiple ways to go about using theories for the purposes of interpretation. Some of these ways are more formal than others, such as the use of structured-focused analyses or simulations that rest on a quantitative foundation. Others, such as more informal trial-and-error approaches take a more rough-and-ready approach to methodology but can nevertheless accumulate knowledge through the evolution of best practices.

One of the major points, however, that I have made about the application of theory to the "real world" is that it is not always a one-way street that simply uses theory as an interpretative lens. Just as important, in many cases, is the feedback that a researcher receives when he or she finds out that reality rarely accords neatly with theory. When reality and theory diverge, it is clear that one or the other bears closer scrutiny.

I have emphasized throughout this book that the conclusions that researchers often reach are incomplete or flawed. There are few research projects that yield undeniable conclusions. Understanding methodology, however, not only provides us with a better understanding of how to tackle original research but also helps us figure out what questions to ask about earlier research and how to go about answering them.

DISCUSSION QUESTIONS

6.1 Make a list of "-isms" that you might have heard or learned about in the past. Pick one and describe how it might be used to better understand a historical or contemporary event or to make predictions about the future. What subjects would the theory focus on?

6.2 Simulations come in many forms, but they differ from standard "tests." Which of the following represent simulations and which do not? Why or why not?

   a. A physicist projects the path of asteroids in the solar system to predict which ones pose a danger to Earth.

b. A psychiatrist uses images of the brain to determine why some individuals are more aggressive than others.

c. Engineers in an automotive plant use crash test dummies to determine how a high-speed crash causes injuries in a particular model of car.

d. A nutritionist analyzes the results of questionnaires about lifestyle habits and concludes that TV watching is associated with increased obesity.

e. A political scientist uses a model of past electoral behavior to forecast the results of an upcoming election.

6.3 Consider how you have learned the things in life that you have learned. What other ways did you learn about the world that did not involve research? How much of a role has purposeful research played in learning what you know? How does the information we gain from research differ from other ways of gaining knowledge?

Afterword

In the preface to this book, I mentioned that one of the major reasons I decided to take on this project was because, as an early graduate student, I could never quite find a book about methodology that worked for me. The books I found were either focused solely on narrow areas of research or were daunting, voluminous tomes that attempted to address every methodological detail. In this book, I have attempted to find a middle ground, providing an overview of many aspects of research while attempting to avoid being bogged down in lengthy discussions of particular topics that an interested reader could explore elsewhere.

Another experience that motivated me to write this book was my earliest experience of teaching methodology to upper-level undergraduates. As a substitute for the regular methodology professor at the time, I was tasked with following his syllabus and using his reading list for the class. As indicated by the evaluations at the end of the class, the students were, as a whole, "miserable" and "bored," and a few suggested in not-so-kind words that I be asked to find work elsewhere.

I spent a lot of time thinking in subsequent semesters, at a different university, about how to go about presenting methodology in a less "cookie-cutter" fashion. I wanted to get students to think about methodology as a coherent and interesting exercise in critical thinking and discovery rather than a mindless box of tools representing poorly understood means to poorly understood ends.

An important part of the process of making research more approachable to students involved developing a model to help tie it all together. Part of what makes research so abstract for students is the fact that texts about research are often presented as disjointed chapters, full of information but with seemingly little relation to one another. Figure 1.1 is a simple product of years of thought—an admittedly imperfect but straightforward attempt to display the interconnections between different areas of research that students, or scholars, might pursue.

Over the past several years, students have continued to take part in the development of this text, providing me with valuable feedback about the parts they have and have not understood. At the same time, other scholars have offered their own feedback, and for better or for worse, it has been instructive as well.

I work in a mixed department of historians and social scientists, which has informed the broad approach to methodology found herein. One historian once told me that some historians openly reject the idea of methodological discussion. Another told me that in history, the path to understanding is achieved by presenting "evidence by argumentation."

These views are not at all uncharacteristic of approaches to understanding often taken in the more qualitative scholarly fields. Some questions are best approached by researchers who are more interested in what they are learning rather than how they should be learning it. Exploratory, descriptive, applied, and interpretative research can often bypass considerations of validity and reliability that typify more quantitatively oriented research. Qualitative conclusions can sometimes only be evaluated as they evolve through argumentation. What this book has to offer such qualitative scholars, however, is a better idea of how to frame their work, a better idea of how it relates to the work of others, and the boundaries and limitations of any causal conclusions drawn.

One of the main points of this work is that all research, qualitative and quantitative, tends to have limitations. Another qualitative scholar pointed out the boundaries of this work when, on reviewing an earlier draft, he asked why I was not spending more time discussing "ethnography" and "discourse analysis." Another scholar, a quantitative-minded psychologist drawing on his own experiences, asked why I did not have a more up-front discussion of experimental methodology. The number of specific research topics I have not covered, or not covered in great depth, far exceeds the number of topics that I have.

Recently, for example, as a method of cross-checking the extensive glossary in this work, I browsed through the excellent *SAGE Dictionary of Social Research Methods* (Jupp, 2006). Of the entries in the *SAGE Dictionary*, only roughly 10% to 20% appear in the glossary found in this book, and vice versa. In other words, there are many topics in research that have been left out of both volumes in the name of conciseness and brevity. Since I attempt to encompass some aspects of research in the humanities and natural sciences as well as the social world, it is clear that this text represents only the tip of the iceberg when it comes to learning how research is done. Researchers throughout the ages have taught us not only what we now know but also how much we will always have to learn.

As an introduction to many of the concepts across a variety of research fields, however, this book has succeeded if it has made you feel more comfortable with some of the main issues and approaches involved in the discovery and creation of knowledge. The rest is up to you.

Glossary

Action research (6): Similar to the concept of *praxis*, although less theoretically grounded, connotes the acquisition and refinement of knowledge in a hands-on, practical environment.

ANOVA (5): Statistical "analysis of variance" used commonly when an independent variable is categorical and a dependent variable is continuous. Often useful when a difference-of-means tests is not, because the independent variable can assume more than two values. Commonly used to analyze experimental data where the independent variable is usually categorical (control, Treatment 1, Treatment 2, etc.) while the dependent variable is often continuous.

Applied theory/Applied theoretical research (1, 6): The use of theory to help understand or solve problems in "real-world" situations or case studies. Those applying theory also contribute to "research" by providing feedback as to whether or not theories adequately address such real-world problems or require further revision.

Autocorrelation (5): Statistical problem that often arises in time-series analysis that is characterized by the correlation of error terms with one another.

Baseline analysis (5): Used in many projects to help better interpret coefficients obtained from regressions with limited dependent variables. The analysis entails setting all independent variables in an equation to baseline values (usually their means for continuous variables and 0 for discrete variables) and then altering the value of one variable at a time and calculating the subsequent change in the dependent variable.

Behavioralism (3): Social science approach that focuses on the quantitative analysis of trends in outwardly observable human behavior rather than on traditional structural-institutionalist or interpretivist theories.

Note: The numbers in parentheses refer to the chapters where discussion of this topic can be found.

Bell curve (2): A normal distribution.

Bivariate statistic (2): Statistic that describes the relationship between the values of two variables.

Case study research (3, 6): Contextual research that examines a contemporary or historical event or process for the purposes of (a) description, (b) theory building, (c) theoretical application to interpret "real-world" events through the lens of theory, and/or (d) evaluating theories to understand how a theory might be extended or revised.

Categorical (or qualitative) variable (4): Discrete variable that takes on nonnumerical values, whether ordinal or nominal.

Causal theory (1): Explanations gleaned inductively or deductively that clarify why and how a single event or multiple events occur. Causal theories range from idiographic explanations of particular situations to nomothetic explanations of universal phenomena.

Census (2): Research that studies characteristics of an entire population by surveying the entire population rather than a sample subset of the population.

Ceterus parabus (5): Latin for "all things equal" that is used to indicate that a variable's influence is being considered in isolation from all other variables (whose values are considered as "held constant").

Chi-square testing (5): Method commonly used to determine the level of statistical significance in cross-tabulation analysis between or among categorical variables.

Classic experimental design (4): A method of creating data characterized by the random selection of subjects, division of selected subjects into treatment and (usually) a control group, and the direct manipulation of the independent variable (the treatment) by a researcher. Data gathered through classic experimentation are more amenable to analysis because they ideally alleviate problems caused by sample selection bias, omitted variable bias, and endogeneity.

Classification (1, 2): The organization of information to aid in the recognition of patterns and the development of causal inferences.

Coefficient (5): In regression analysis, number that is derived that indicates the expected magnitude of the change in the dependent variable values for each change in an independent variable's values. Often denoted with a β.

Collinearity (5): Statistical problem that arises when the values of an independent variable are linearly correlated, to a greater or lesser degree, with the values of another independent variable. The greater the "overlap" in values between variables, the more values that are essentially "wasted" for the purposes of analysis. If two values are perfectly collinear, then no conclusions can be drawn concerning which is influencing the dependent variable.

Comparative methodologies (3, 6): Primarily a method of theory building that entails the careful selection of cases to eliminate sources of explanation that might challenge the main theoretical argument being developed by a researcher. Includes most-similar case designs ("controlled comparisons") and different systems designs.

Composite variable (4): A variable whose values are determined as a function of the values of other, generally more directly measurable, variables. Many constructs/concepts are composite variables.

Conceptual mapping (2): The process of diagramming an unobservable construct such that its constituent subconcepts, or elements, are logically organized in a manner that is exhaustive and nonredundant.

Conceptualization (1, 2): The process of defining "latent," intangible concepts by logically deducing the nonoverlapping elements that comprise the main concept of interest.

Concurrent validity (4): Type of criterion-related validity in which a variable's measured values are judged by their degree of correlation with a similar (reflecting the same concept) variable's values that are operationalized at roughly the same time as the first variable.

Conditional logic (3): Logical, deductive form that states that if certain conditions are met then certain consequences will follow.

Constant (or y-intercept) (5): In a regression, it indicates the expected value of the dependent variable if all of the coefficients or the sum of the other terms equaled zero. Used for statistical calculations of expected values of dependent variables but usually not of primary interest to a researcher because it does not indicate anything about the relationship between any particular independent and dependent variable as coefficients do. Often denoted with an α or a β_0.

Construct (2): A variable that is composed of "latent," nonobservable elements that may be further broken down or operationalized. Used here as synonymous to the word *concept*.

Construct validity (4): The degree to which the conceptualization and measurement of a construct is thought to correspond with empirical reality.

Constructivist (1): Term describing the branch of learning theory that asserts that social meaning is constructed through the process of interpersonal interactions.

Content analysis (2): The method and procedures through which the words, images, and concepts of recorded information are coded for the purposes of quantitative analysis.

Content validity (4): The degree to which the process of conceptualizing a latent variable seems to accurately and exhaustively reflect the constituent elements making up the variable.

Contingency table (5): Table that displays the joint frequencies of two or more variables.

Continuous variable (4): Variable that can be broken down decimally and thus can take an infinite number of values within a particular range.

Controlling (3, 5): Holding one factor "constant" so that other variables can be studied under the condition that all other things are equal. In classic experiments, a control group is used as a basis of comparison with treatment groups. In statistics, control is used to overcome omitted variable problems by eliminating the effect of variations in potentially confounding variables.

Convenience sampling (2): Nonprobabilistic selection of research subjects on the basis of easy accessibility.

Convergent validity (4): Criterion for judging a concept's operationalized values by correlating them with the values of a presumably related variable and seeing if there is a strong, positive correlation.

Correlation analysis (2): A statistical method of measuring the strength and direction of the linear association between (usually two) variables. By far the most common measurement is "Pearson's product–moment correlation coefficient," which is denoted with an r that ranges from -1 to $+1$ and indicates the strength of the correlation between the values.

Counterfactual reasoning (3): Causal argument that something would occur or would have occurred had conditions been different. When a particular event has a particular outcome, counterfactual reasoning is used to make a logically consistent argument by artificially "creating" alternate values of independent and dependent values for the sake of comparison with those observed.

Covert observation (2): First-person observation of subjects by a researcher who does not divulge his or her identity. Ethical considerations may arise for certain types of covert projects.

Cox regression model (5): Type of survival model that involves the calculation of a "baseline hazard function" that is used to understand how event "failure rates" vary over time.

Criterion-related validity (4): The degree to which the value measurements assigned to a latent variable correlate with external empirical data that one would think would be related to the same underlying concept.

Critical (or "crucial") case studies (6): Case studies that affirm or discredit universal or deterministic theoretical claims.

Critical test (1, 5): Definitive, nonstatistical, nonprobabilistic test of a deterministic or universal phenomenon to establish whether the phenomenon is likely to exist or not. Critical tests are more common in the natural sciences, within which phenomena tend to be more universal in nature than in the social sciences.

Critical theory (3): Approach in the social sciences that focuses on structural relations between groups and advocates an active role for researchers in challenging inequitable power structures on behalf of the disadvantaged.

Cross-sectional data (5): Data that include values of one or more variables for different subjects at a particular point in time.

Cross-tabulation analysis (5): Type of statistical analysis commonly employed to better understand the relationship between categorical variables.

Cybernetics (6): The study of how informational feedback loops influence behavior.

Data (1, 2): Information, as interpreted by a researcher, about the factual world that is obtained through observation or experimentation.

Deductive reasoning (3): The development of causal or descriptive explanations through logical and/or mathematical reasoning that is based on assumptions, axioms, or other preexisting "given" information.

Dependent variable (4): Variable whose values are theorized to be influenced by the values of one or more specified independent variables.

Descriptive research (1, 2): Research that seeks answers to noncausal factual questions by explaining the characteristics of data and events and answering questions like "who?" "'what?" "where?" and "when?"

Descriptive statistics (2): Statistics that reflect the characteristics of a sample of data such as mean and standard deviation. It is usually univariate in nature, although correlations and cross-tabulations are examples of bi- or multivariate descriptive statistics.

Dichotomous variable (4): A variable that only assumes two potential values, often expressed as 1 or 0.

Difference-of-means tests (5): Statistical test commonly used when one variable (usually specified as an independent variable) is dichotomous and the other (usually specified as dependent) is continuous. Using a *t* test, a researcher can determine whether the dependent variable values associated with one value of the independent variable are statistically different from those associated with the other value of the independent variable.

Direct observation (2): First person observation of a phenomenon that allows for the collection and recording of data through a researcher's own senses.

Discrete quantitative variable (4): Variable that can only take specific values, generally whole numbers, within a particular range. It is generally associated with "event-count"-type variables.

Discrete variable (4): Variable that can only take specific values, whether quantitative or categorical.

Divergent validity (4): Criterion for judging a concept's operationalized values by correlating them with the values of a variable that are expected to represent an opposite effect and seeing if there is a strong, negative correlation.

Dummy variable (4): Type of dichotomous variable that is used even though more precise information about the values of a variable is, at least in principle, available.

Effect size (5): The amount of change, as determined through statistical analysis, in one variable that a researcher would expect to witness in relationship to another variable. Only really useful to know if a relationship is also found to be statistically significant.

Empirical (1): Information that is measurable and either directly or indirectly observable.

Endogeneity (2): In statistics, bias that occurs because the values of a coefficient or variable are systematically related to the error terms in an analysis. Examples include omitted variable and simultaneity/reverse causality bias.

Episodic records (2): Primary sources such as diaries, speeches, or video footage that reflect information recorded at a particular time and place.

Error (5): In a regression analysis, the amount of deviation of a sample point from the "true" relationship between independent and dependent variables. As relationships between variables tend to be probabilistic rather than deterministic, error will almost always exist due to random factors that influence particular outcomes. Denoted by ε. See also *residual*.

Eta-squared (5): Used as an indicator of "magnitude" in ANOVA analysis, this statistic reveals how much of the variance of the values of the dependent variable results from variance in the independent variables.

Ethnography (2, 3): Research that studies cultural or social groups to find and describe beliefs, values, and attitudes that structure the behavior, language, and interactions of the group.

Experimentation (1, 4): Method of creating data through the structured intervention of a researcher, who creates the conditions for subject interactions (qualitative experimentation) or follows a process of random selection, random assignment, and treatment administration (classic experimentation). Data gathered from classic experimentation are more useful for analysis and testing than those gathered through passive observation because issues like sample selection bias, omitted variable bias, and simultaneity/reverse causality bias are mitigated or eliminated.

External validity (4): The degree to which research findings obtained in one setting are applicable to other settings.

F **test (5):** Statistic commonly associated with the determination of statistical significance in ANOVA analysis. An F test calculates a p value based on the ratio of the variance between categories to the variance of the observations within each category.

Factor analysis (4): Method of statistical analysis that determines the properties of unobserved concepts by calculating variations in related variables that can be observed.

Field experiment (4): Study that utilizes experimental-type techniques in "real world," rather than structured, laboratory environments.

Focus group (2): The practice of interviewing numerous individuals at the same time in order to gain their perspectives and to raise new lines of inquiry about particular issues. Like any type of interview, the opinions expressed in a focus group sample cannot be said to validly reflect the opinions of a larger population.

Game theory (3): Formal, deductive use of mathematics designed to understand the strategic interactions of actors seeking to maximize their own welfare ("utility").

Gauss–Markov assumptions (5): Set of conditions that must be met such that OLS coefficients represent the "best linear unbiased estimators."

Goodness-of-fit statistic (5): Statistic indicating the percentage of the spread, or variance, of data points that can be explained by the values of the independent variables within a given model.

Grounded theory (2): Detailed methodology first described by Glaser and Strauss in 1967, which emphasizes the cyclical nature of data collection and theory building. Just as data collection leads to theoretical insights, development of theory guides the process of further data collection.

Hawthorne effect (4): The influence that the knowledge that he or she is part of an experiment can have on subject behavior.

Hazard ratio (5): Output of a survival model that denotes how a dependent variable's "failure rate" increases or decreases for a given change in unit of a particular independent variable.

Heteroscedasticity (5): Term indicating that the random errors of the functional relationship between independent and dependent variables are dispersed differently depending on the values of the variables.

History (4): Term used to describe a threat to a project's internal validity that involves something external and uncontrollable happening in the middle of a project that influences subject responses.

Hypothesis (1, 4): Testable proposition deduced from a theoretical model that states what one would expect to witness empirically if the relations specified in a model are correct.

Idiographic (3): Latin for "particularistic," refers to research questions, methodologies, and theory that focuses on phenomena that occur in a specific context and environment.

Independent variable (4): Variable whose values are theorized to causally influence the values of another variable that is specified as a dependent variable.

Indirect observation (2): Observation of evidence that allows a researcher to infer information about an unobserved phenomenon.

Inductive reasoning (3): The development of causal or descriptive explanations based on direct or indirect empirical evidence.

Inference (1): Information that a researcher believes exists even though he or she cannot directly observe the data in question. Inferences can be descriptive or causal in nature and arrived at either inductively or deductively.

Inferential statistics (2, 5): Statistics that represent estimates of population characteristics or trends between variables that are derived from probabilistic calculations that are based on available sample data. Estimates of statistical significance are inferential statistics that are central to hypothesis testing.

Institutional review boards (2): Committees that are formed at research institutions and tasked with evaluating the ethical acceptability of studies involving human subjects. They are also commonly known as human subject committees.

Institutionalism (3): Branch of structuralism that focuses on the role played by laws, organizations, and bureaucracies in determining social and political outcomes.

Intercoder reliability (2): A measurement, often expressed as a correlation coefficient, that indicates the degree to which the coding of multiple parties conducting content analysis agree with one another.

Interitem correlation (4): The calculated correlation of different variables generally with the intention to determine whether the variable values reflect similar elements of a concept. Often a correlation matrix is created to display the correlations between multiple variables in order to see which seem more closely related than others.

Internal validity (4): The degree to which the design and process of research is likely to lead to accurate answers to the research questions being investigated within a particular research setting.

Interpretivist approaches (1, 3): Approaches in the social sciences that attempt to describe and understand individual perceptions and small group interactions.

Interval measurement (4): Measurement in units that can be described in terms of their distance from one another but cannot be used in multiplication and subtraction. When interval units are being used, the value "zero" does not truly represent the absence of the thing being measured, such as zero on the Celsius or Fahrenheit scale.

Interview (2): The process of gathering information by seeking the opinions of nonrandomly selected people or groups. The small-scale, qualitative nature of interviewing allows for an in-depth understanding of individual characteristics and perspectives, but it is generally not appropriate for estimating more general opinion trends.

Law of large numbers (4): Central concept in statistical reasoning that reflects the fact that the values become closer to their expected distribution as more data about a phenomenon are collected.

Literature review (2, 3): Both a process and a product of examining secondary source research in areas associated with a researchers subject of interest. As a process, reviewing literature helps researchers come up with research questions of their own and situate their own research within the context of related efforts and findings. As a product, literature reviews (even if not labeled directly as such) are included in most studies so that readers understand how a researcher's work differs from or extends the work of other research.

Logit regression (5): Type of regression often conducted, along with probit regression, when a dependent variable is dichotomous.

Longitudinal data (5): Data that include the measurement of multiple variable values for the same subject over time.

Macrolevel theory (3): "Grand" theory of causality that is often structural and universalistic in nature.

Margin of error (2): The amount, plus or minus, that a value of a variable obtained from a sample is expected to deviate from the true population value of that variable. Unless otherwise expressed, margin of error generally implies that the true population value will lie within the margin of error of a sample 95% of the time.

Maturation (4): The term used to describe a threat to a project's internal validity that involves changes to the characteristics of subjects during the course of a study that might affect the conclusions drawn from the research.

Mediated data collection (2): The process of collecting research information from written or recorded sources.

Methodology (1): The manner in which a researcher goes about researching a question in the pursuit of valid answers. Methodology can be thought of as an overarching approach that is composed of sets of more specific research methods.

Microlevel theory (3): Largely synonymous with qualitative theory, describes causal explanations involving human perceptions and motivations and smaller-scale human and natural events.

Midlevel theory (3): Causal explanations that seek to understand trends in the relationships among variables concerning a particular population of subjects. Characterized by inductive research and often statistical in nature.

Model (1): A simplified representation of theory that has been stripped down to show the essential interactions among its variables.

Mortality (4): Term used to describe a threat to a project's internal validity that occurs when subjects drop out of a study for reasons that might be correlated with the outcome of the study.

Multicollinearity (5): The same as *collinearity*, except that variable values are correlated with a linear function of two or more variables.

Natural experiment (4): Study that involves the use of natural or social changes in the environment that are beyond the control of the subjects of study as a substitute for researcher intervention in setting values of independent variables.

Negative binomial regression (5): Type of regression commonly used, along with negative binomial regression, when a dependent variable is quantitative and discrete. It is commonly associated with modeling the causes of variables representing "event counts."

Negative relationship (5): Relationship between variables in which the expected increase in the values of one variable is related to an expected decrease in the values of another variable.

Nominal variable (4): Variable that takes on nonnumerical values that cannot be logically ordered.

Nomothetic (3): Latin for "proposition of the law," refers to research questions, methodologies, and theory that focus on understanding universal causal trends.

Nonparticipatory observation (2): First person observation in which a researcher in the field accompanies the subjects being studied but does not engage in their activities.

Nonprobabilistic sampling (2): Nonrandom sampling conducted for reasons other than the desire to extrapolate characteristics of a general population from a sample. It often takes the form of focus groups or other types of multiple-subject interviewing.

Normal distribution (2): A common type of symmetric distribution of a variable's values whose properties include the fact that the mode, median, and mean of the variable values are all the same. Like other statistical distributions, the normal distribution is based on a mathematical function that enables its use in a variety of statistical calculations.

Null hypothesis (5): Hypothesis that would suggest a lack of statistical relationship between variables. When empirical evidence seems to verify a causal relationship, one can say that the null hypothesis (of no relationship) has been rejected and the "alternate hypothesis" of a relationship accepted.

Observation (1): Can be defined as encompassing a variety of direct and indirect ways of collecting data through nonexperimental means or, more literally, as the collection of data through "firsthand" experiences.

Omitted variable bias (2, 4, 5): Problem arising from the analysis of observational data, whereby the influence of a "lurking" or "confounding" variable that influences both an independent variable as well as the dependent variable is not considered. Omitting such variables from an analysis inflates the apparent effect of an independent variable if the omitted variable is positively correlated and reduces the apparent effect if the omitted variable is negatively correlated.

Ontological (3): Term describing the study of and underlying assumptions associated with the nature of reality. Positivist-minded scholars focus on the search for understanding within an "objective" reality while interpretivists investigate reality as it is created through socially constructed understandings and subjective individual perception.

Operationalization (1, 4): The process of making a concept/construct "operational" or usable for quantitative analysis by breaking down a latent variable into measurable components or using a measurable proxy variable that closely represents the concept or interest.

Ordered logit and probit regression (5): Common types of regression analysis utilized when a dependent variable takes on ordinal values (rather than dichotomous values as in "simple" logit and probit).

Ordinal variable (4): Variable that takes on values that can be logically ordered, such as "small, medium, large," but whose numerical distance from one another is not expressed.

Ordinary least squares (OLS) (5): Common type of regression analysis utilized when a dependent variable takes values that are continuous.

Panel data (5): Data that combine longitudinal and cross-sectional data into a data set that includes multiple observations of multiple subjects over time.

Parsimony (3): Characteristic of an explanation that explains the "most with the least." All things being equal, the simplest theory is the best theory.

Participatory observation (2): First-person observation in which a researcher in the field takes part in the activities of the subjects being studied.

Phenomenalism (2, 3): An approach that seeks to describe and understand individual perceptions with the assumption that mental constructs and reality are largely inseparable.

Poisson regression (5): Type of regression commonly used, along with negative binomial regression, when a dependent variable is quantitative and discrete. It is commonly associated with modeling the causes of variables representing "event counts."

Polling (2): A simple form of survey research that involves a single or small number of questions.

Population (2): The entire group about which a researcher is interested in drawing conclusions. When a population is large, researchers often select a representative sample from which they may infer characteristics about a broader population.

Positive relationship (5): Relationship between variables in which the expected increase in the values of one variable are related to an expected increase in the values of another variable.

Positivism (3): Epistemological approach to knowledge that asserts that knowledge can only be accumulated through the study of empirical, verifiable phenomena.

Praxis (6): The process of putting theory into action "in the field" for the purposes of evaluating the appropriateness of a theory in "real-world" settings.

Predictive validity (4): Type of criterion-related validity in which a variable's measured values are judged by their degree of correlation with a similar (reflecting the same concept) variable's values that are operationalized at a future date. A classic example is the degree to which college entrance exams correlate with student grades once students are in college.

Primary sources (2): "Noninterpretative" recorded sources of information that generally recount firsthand description information, but whose main purpose is not to draw causal conclusions.

Probabilistic sampling (2): Selection of a representative sample based on the principle that every member of a population has an equal chance of being selected. It makes use of random selection and (sometimes) preexisting information about the distribution of characteristics in a population.

Probit regression (5): Type of regression often conducted, along with logit regression, when a dependent variable is dichotomous.

Proportional reduction of error (5): Statistics indicating the "magnitude' of the relationship between categorical variables that are commonly used in cross-tabulation analysis. Indicate how much better the values of one categorical variable can be predicted given the information provided by the other variable(s)' values.

p value (5): Probability that the observed change in the values (covariance) of two variables would occur if random values had been assigned to each variable. The lower the p value, the more likely something else other than random chance, such as a theorized causal mechanism or an omitted variable, is influencing the relationship between the variables.

Qualitative (1): Research that involves a small number of cases (i.e., small-n research) with the goal of collecting and providing descriptive information, gleaning descriptive inferences, developing causal theories, or using causal theories to understand "real-world" events.

Qualitative experiment (2): Type of observational research in which a researcher creates a structured environment to observe the subsequent behavior of subjects within that environment.

Qualitative research (3): Research that focuses on in-depth understanding of the characteristics, relationships, and processes associated with a small number of contexts.

Quantitative (1): Research that involves a large number of cases with the goal of collecting or providing descriptive information, gleaning descriptive inferences, developing causal theories, and/or testing causal theories to determine whether empirical trends in data support established theory.

Quantitative observational data (2): Numerical data that are compiled through direct observation or instruments that allow for a researcher to collect information that is otherwise difficult to access or measure. Such data differ from those which are collected through classic experimentation.

Quantitative research (3): Research that focuses on the description, measurement, and testing of large amounts of data to uncover behavioral regularities.

Quasi-experiment (4): Study that utilizes elements of classic design such as random selection and/or researcher intervention but generally, for practical reasons, does not entail random assignment to treatment or control groups. As defined in this text, quasi-experimental design should be thought of as more structured than a qualitative experimental design, while "falling short" of a true classic design.

Quota sampling (2): Nonprobabilistic sampling that seeks out (nonrandomly) a range of different characteristics among subjects to approximate representativeness.

Ratio measurement (4): Measurement of a variable's values such that the values taken represent real numerical "amounts" that can be used in mathematical operations involving division and multiplication.

Rational choice (3): A deductive approach to social theory that explains expected individual and group outcomes by assuming that actors will, when given choices, act on a specific set of preferences in such a way as to maximize their expected utility.

Realism (3): Approach to knowledge that suggests that while not all phenomena are empirical in nature, repeated analysis and study can nevertheless reveal a great deal about social and natural events (*note:* this is one of many definitions of "realism" found in research).

Regression analysis (5): Family of statistical tests whose aim is to determine the expected values of dependent variables conditional on the values of one or more independent variables. The analysis entails deriving the magnitude of the relationship of each independent variable to the dependent variable as well as determining whether the relationship is statistically significant—all while controlling for the values of other independent variables if they exist. It is most useful when at least one of the independent variables is continuous.

Regression to the mean (4): Phenomenon whereby the further away the value of a dependent variable is from the variable mean, the more likely that value will subsequently move closer to the mean value in the future due to the "averaging out" of random factors responsible for temporarily larger or smaller values taken by the variable.

Reliability (4): Characteristic of research or variable measurement that describes the degree to which the process and results of the research process are replicable in further studies.

Research (1): Systematic and intentional effort to answer questions and learn more about a specific subject.

Residual (5): Related to the concept of "error," the amount of deviation of a sample point from the estimated (rather than unobserved "true") relationship between independent and dependent variables. Denoted by μ. See also *error*.

Response rate (2): The percentage of those solicited to participate in a survey who end up taking part in the survey.

Robust (5): Term used to describe a statistical finding that remains consistent even when alternate methods, operationalizations, or other assumptions are employed in an analysis.

r-squared (r^2) value (2, 5): Also known as the "coefficient of determination," an r-squared value indicates how much of the covariance of variables is explained by a particular model (e.g., a linear correlation or regression model). The unexplained variance is residual error. Were a model a perfect fit for the data, the r-squared value would equal 1.0, and were observed data completely random, it would equal 0.

Running records (2): Data, such as hospital records or online data sets, that have been intentionally compiled over a period of time and may be used to analyze quantitative trends.

Sample (2): A subset of a larger population. If the characteristics of a sample are to truly represent the underlying characteristics of a population, every member of the population must have an equal chance of being selected in the sample.

Sample error (2): A statistical calculation that indicates how accurate or inaccurate a researcher is likely to be when calculating a quantitative characteristic of a sample population and extrapolating it to the population from which the sample was drawn.

Scalar variable (4): A variable whose values consist of only a single element (i.e., not a composite variable).

Secondary sources (2): Interpretative works that analyze primary sources or other types of descriptive information.

Selecting on the dependent variable (4): Literally speaking, small-n research design in which cases for study are chosen according to their dependent variable values. It connotes, however, designs in which cases are carelessly chosen without regard to the relation between dependent variables and independent variables or in which all the dependent variable values (outcomes) are the same, making causal inference impossible (outside of "different systems" designs).

Selection bias (2): Problem that arises when a sample is chosen in such a fashion that it will not accurately represent a population, thus yielding inaccurate conclusions. It is also known as sampling bias.

Simple random sampling (2): Sample selection that occurs through the selection of population members purely at random.

Simulation (6): Research design that attempts to predict outcomes based on the behavior of "made-up" (predicted, for instance, rather than empirically observed) data that are introduced into the framework of a preexisting model.

Simultaneity/reverse causality bias (2, 4, 5): Theoretical problem encountered when a theorized dependent variable causally influences a theorized independent variable in whole or in part.

Snowball sampling (2): Sampling through "networks" that are generally created through references provided as part of an interviewing process.

Spurious relationship (3): A relationship between two variables that is wrongly inferred due to the presence of an omitted variable or because the relationship is coincidental.

Standard error of the estimate (in a regression equation) (5): Measure involving a regression coefficient's expected accuracy that involves taking the square root of the ratio of the total amount of error (SSR) to the number of observations.

Statistical significance (5): The benchmark probability at which values of one variable vary strongly enough with those of another variable that a nonrandom relationship can be inferred. $p < .05$ is a common standard convention for statistical significance that suggests that there is less than a 5% chance that the relationship of the observed values of two variables would occur through random chance.

Stratified sampling (2): Type of probabilistic sampling that is employed when preexisting information exists concerning the size of different subgroups within a population. By dividing those subgroups into proportional "strata" and then sampling randomly among those strata, a researcher can overcome biases caused by different response rates as well as decrease random sample error.

Structuralism (3): Theoretical approach in the social sciences that suggests that the behavior of social actors is channeled in particular directions through constraints on and incentives toward certain actions. Structures are often cultural, political, institutional, or economic in nature.

Structured observation (2): First-person research that involves a focused search on the part of the researcher who enters a research environment with a definitive idea of the type of data being sought and established procedures for uncovering the desired data.

Structured-focused analysis (6): Theoretical application conducted by focusing on a limited number of specific issues within a single or small number of cases to better understand the phenomenon in question while shedding light on potential shortcomings, revisions, or extensions of the original theoretical framework being employed.

Survey instrument (2): A questionnaire.

Survey research (2): Research designed to extrapolate characteristics of a general population through the use of probabilistically (randomly) selected samples. It usually refers to studies of public opinion that are obtained through the distribution and retrieval of questionnaires.

Survival analysis (5): Type of regression used when a researcher is interested in the influence that independent variables will have on the likelihood of an event occurring over time.

Syllogism (3): Logical construction used in deductive reasoning that bases a conclusion on "major" and "minor" premises.

***t* test (5):** Type of statistical test used to determine whether the values of two variables can be considered significantly different from one another (i.e., not random chance), given the values themselves and the number of observations considered. It is commonly used in difference-of-means tests and when determining the statistical significance of coefficients in linear regression.

Taxonomy (1, 2): A schema for the sensible division of empirical information.

Theoretical argument (3): A researcher's presentation of theory, which may be judged on the strength of that researcher's methodologies, underlying assumptions, logical connections, and his or her elimination of alternate theories, among other factors.

Theoretical refinement (1, 6): The process of revising a theory based on new understandings that are gleaned from the process of data collection, including the lessons learned from theoretical application. The perpetual process of theoretical refinement defines the cyclical nature of the research process as a whole.

Trial-and-error approach (1, 6): "Evolutionary" approach to knowledge that entails applying theoretical ideas to "real-world" situations, obtaining feedback about the effectiveness of the theory in helping cope with such situations, and revising the theory based on the knowledge gained from experience.

Triangulation (3): The use of multiple methodological approaches to gain understanding of different aspects of a phenomenon.

Typology (1, 2, 4): A schema for classifying latent, nonempirical characteristics of concepts according to the elements that they do or do not have in common.

Univariate statistic (2): Statistics such as mean, median, and mode that describe the properties of the values taken by a particular variable.

Unstructured observation (2): First-person research that begins as exploratory in nature and involves the willingness of a researcher to adapt his or her methods and focus of interest as new information is uncovered.

Validity (4): Characteristic of research or variable measurement suggesting the degree to which (a) a research project is designed to accurately address the research question under investigation or (b) a variable is measured such that the values it assumes accurately capture the concept that the variable purports to measure.

Verstehen (3): The term used in qualitative research to connote efforts to acquire a deep and contextual understanding of the motivations and perceptions of those being studied.

References

Abbott, A. (2004). *Methods of discovery: Heuristics for the social sciences*. New York, NY: W. W. Norton.

Achen, C. H., & Snidal, D. (1989). Rational deterrence theory and comparative case studies. *World Politics, 41*, 143–169.

Aldert, V., Edward, K., & Bull, R. (2001). People's insights into their own behavior and speech content while lying. *British Journal of Psychology, 92*, 373–390.

Alvarez, W. (1997). *"T. Rex" and the crater of doom*. Princeton, NJ: Princeton University Press.

Anckar, C. (2004). *Determinants of the death penalty: A comparative study of the world*. New York, NY: Routledge.

Bailey, K. (1994). *Typologies and taxonomies: An introduction to classification techniques*. Thousand Oaks, CA: Sage.

Bell, J. (1993). *Doing your own research project: A guide to first-time researchers in education and social sciences* (2nd ed.). Buckingham, England: Open University Press.

Bernard, R. (2000). *Social research methods: Qualitative and quantitative approaches*. Thousand Oaks, CA: Sage.

Bernard, R. (2002). *Research methods in anthropology: Qualitative and quantitative methods*. Walnut Creek, CA: AltaMira Press.

Brown, M. (1989, May 3). Physicists debunk claims of a new kind of fusion. *The New York Times*. Retrieved from http://partners.nytimes.com/library/national/science/050399sci-cold-fusion.html

Bunge, M. (1996). *Finding philosophy in social science*. New Haven, CT: Yale University Press.

Camino, L., Zelden, S., & Payne-Jackson, A. (1995). *Basics of qualitative interviews and focus groups*. Washington, DC: Center for Youth Development and Policy Research, Academy for Educational Development.

Cioffi-Revilla, C. (1983). The political reliability of Italian governments: A survival model. *American Political Science Review, 78*, 318–337.

Cohen, P. A. (1981). Student ratings of instruction and student achievement: A meta-analysis of multisection validity studies. *Review of Educational Research, 41*, 281–310.

Collier, P., & Hoeffler, A. (2002). Greed and grievance in civil wars. *Oxford Economic Papers, 56*, 563–595.

Conway, M., Grabe, M. E., & Grieves, M. (2007). Villains, victims and the virtuous in Bill O'Reilly's "No-spin" zone: Revisiting world war propaganda techniques. *Journalism Studies, 8*, 197–223.

Coppedge, M. (2002, April). *Theory building and hypothesis testing: Large- vs. small-n research on science association.* Paper presented at the annual meeting of the Midwest Political Science Association, Chicago, IL. Retrieved from http://nd.edu/~mcoppedg/crd/mpsacopp02.pdf

Cresswell, J. W. (1998). *Qualitative inquiry and research design: Choosing among five approaches.* Thousand Oaks, CA: Sage.

Crichlow, S. (2002). The effect of members' personality traits on congressional trade voting. *Journal of Conflict Resolution, 46,* 693–711.

Crichlow, S. (2002). Legislators' personality traits and congressional support for free trade. *Journal of Conflict Resolution, 46*(5), 693–711.

Dobson, P. (1999, December). *Approaches to theory use in interpretive case studies: A critical realist perspective.* Paper presented at the 10th Australasian conference on information systems, Victoria University of Wellington, New Zealand.

Douglass, D. H., Clader, B. D., Christy, J. R., Michaels, P. J., & Belsley, D. A. (2003). Test for harmful collinearity among predictor variables used in modeling global climate change. *Climate Research, 24,* 15–18.

Durden, G., & Ellis, L. (2003). Is student attendance a proxy variable for student motivation in an economics class: An empirical analysis. *International Social Science Review, 78,* 42–46.

Durkheim, E. (2006). *On suicide.* London, England: Penguin Books.

Eckstein, H. (1975). Case study and theory in political science. In F. I. Greenstein & N. W. Polsby (Eds.), *Handbook of political science* (pp. 94–137). Reading, MA: Addison-Wesley.

Fearon, J. D. (1991). Counterfactuals and hypothesis testing in the social sciences. *World Politics, 43,* 169–195.

Fearon, J. D., & Laitin, D. D. (2003). Ethnicity, insurgency, and civil war. *American Political Science Review, 97,* 75–90.

Fenno, R. F. (1978). *Home style: House members in their districts.* New York, NY: HarperCollins.

Flyvbjerg, B. (2006). Five misunderstandings about case-study research. *Qualitative Inquiry, 12,* 219–245.

Fontana, A., & Frey, J. (1994). "Interviewing: The art of science." In N. K. Denzin & Y. K. Lincoln (Eds.), *The handbook of qualitative research* (pp. 361–376). Thousand Oaks, CA: Sage.

Friedman, M. (1953). *Essays in positive economics.* Chicago, IL: University of Chicago Press.

George, A. L., & Bennett, A. (2005). *Case studies and theory development in the social sciences.* Cambridge, MA: MIT Press.

Gerber, A. S., & Green, D. P. (2000). The effects of canvassing, telephone calls, and direct mail on voter turnout: A field experiment. *American Political Science Review, 94,* 653–663.

Gerber, A. S., & Green, D. P. (2008). *Get out the vote: How to increase voter turnout* (2nd ed.). Washington, DC: Brookings Institution Press.

Gerring, J. (2004). What is a case study and what is it good for? *American Political Science Review, 98,* 341–354.

Giedion, U., Alfonso, E. A., & Diaz, Y. (2013). *The impact of universal coverage schemes in the developing world: A review of the existing evidence* (UNICO Study Series 25). Washington, DC: World Bank.

Glaser, B. G. (1978). *Theoretical sensitivity.* Mill Valley, CA: Sociology Press.

Glaser, B. G., & Strauss, A. L. (1967). *The discovery of grounded theory: Strategies for qualitative research.* Chicago, IL: Aldine.

Glasersfeld, E. von (2000). Reflections on cybernetics. *Cybernetics and Human Knowing 7*(1), 93–95.

Glazer, A., & Robbins, M. (1985). Congressional responsiveness to constituency change. *American Journal of Political Science, 29,* 259–272.

Glicken, M. (2003). *Social research: A simple guide.* London: Pearson.

Goerres, A., & Prinzen, K. (2012). Using mixed methods for the analysis of individuals: A review of necessary and sufficient conditions and an application to welfare state attitudes. *Quality and Quantity, 46,* 415–450.

Green, D. P., & Shapiro, I. (1994). *The pathologies of rational choice theory: A critique of applications in political science.* New Haven, CT: Yale University Press.

Humphreys, L. (1975). *Tearoom trade: A study of sexual encounters in public places.* Piscataway, NJ: Transaction Books.

Hunter, L., & Leahey, E. (2008). Collaborative research in sociology: Trends and contributing factors. *American Sociologist, 39*(4), 290–306.

Johnson, J., & Reynolds, H. T. (2008). *Political science research methods.* Washington, DC: CQ Press.

Jones, R. A. (1986). *Masters of social theory: Vol. 2. Emile Durkheim: An introduction to four major works.* Beverly Hills, CA: Sage.

Jupp, V. (Ed.). (2006). *The SAGE dictionary of social research methods.* London: Sage.

Lager, A., Jonas, C., & Torssander, J. (2012). Causal effect of education on mortality in a quasi-experiment on 1.2 million Swedes. *Proceedings of the National Academy of Sciences of the United States of America, 109,* 8461–8466.

Lee, R. (2000). *Unobtrusive methods in social research.* Buckingham, England: Open University Press.

Lichbach, M. (2003). *Is rational choice theory all of social science?* Ann Arbor: University of Michigan Press.

Lijphart, A. (1971). Comparative politics and the comparative method. *American Political Science Review, 65,* 682–693.

Lindblom, C. (1959). The science of "Muddling Through." *Public Administration Review, 19,* 79–88.

Loseke, D. (2013). *Thinking methodologically.* Thousand Oaks, CA: Sage.

Lun, J., Mesquita, B., & Smith, B. (2011). Self-and other-presentational styles in the southern and northern United States: An analysis of personal ads. *European Journal of Social Psychology, 41,* 435–445.

Maxwell, J. (1992). Understanding and validity in qualitative research. *Harvard Graduate School of Education, 62,* 279–300.

McLachlan, D., & Justice, J. (2009). A grounded theory of international student well-being. *Journal of Theory Construction and Testing, 13,* 27–32.

Mozaffarian, D., Hao, T., Rimm, E. B., Willett, W. C., & Hu, F. B. (2011). Changes in diet and lifestyle and long-term weight gain in women and men. *New England Journal of Medicine, 364,* 2392–2404.

Munck, G., & Verkuilen, J. (2002). Conceptualizing and measuring democracy. *Comparative Political Studies, 35,* 5–34.

Newman, I., & Benz, C. (1998). *Qualitative-quantitative research methodology: Exploring the interactive continuum.* Carbondale: Southern Illinois University Press.

Patterson, M. M., & Bigler, C. S. (2006). Preschool children's attention to environmental messages about groups: Social categorization and the origins of intergroup bias. *Child Development, 77,* 847–860.

Piff, P., Stancato, D. M., Côté, S., Mendoza-Denton, R., & Keltner, D. (2012). Higher social class predicts increased unethical behavior. *Proceedings of the National Academy of Sciences of the United States of America, 109,* 4086–4091.

Ragin, C. C. (1987). *The comparative method: Moving beyond qualitative and quantitative strategies.* Berkeley: University of California Press.

Ragin, C. C. (2000). *Fuzzy-set social science.* Chicago, IL: University of Chicago Press.

Rose, M., & Baumgartner, F. (2013). Framing the poor: Media coverage and US poverty policy. *Policy Studies Journal, 41,* 22–53.

Rubin, Z. (1970). Measurement of romantic love. *Journal of Personality and Social Psychology, 16,* 265–273.

Ruggeri, A., Gizelis, T., & Dorussen, H. (2011). Events data as Bismarck's sausages? Intercoder reliability, coders' selection, and data quality. *International Interactions, 37,* 340–361.

Sambanis, N. (2004). Using case studies to expand economic models of civil war. *Perspectives on Politics, 2,* 259–279.

Schmidt, W., & Conaway, R. (1998). *Results-oriented interviewing: Principles, practices, and procedures.* Boston, MA: Allyn & Bacon.

Shapiro, I. (2005). *The flight from reality in the human sciences.* Princeton, NJ: Princeton University Press.

Silver, N. (2012). *The signal and the noise: Why so many predictions fail, but some don't.* New York, NY: Penguin Books.

Smith, R. (2002). Should we make political science more of a science or more about politics? *Political Science and Politics, 35,* 199–201.

Strauss, A. (1987). *Qualitative analysis for social scientists.* Cambridge, England: Cambridge University Press.

Teddlie, C., & Tashakkori, A. (2003). Major issues and controversies in the use of mixed methods in the social and behavioral sciences. In C. Teddlie & A. Tashakkori (Eds.), *Handbook of mixed methods in social & behavioral research* (pp. 3–50). Thousand Oaks, CA: Sage.

U.S. Office of Personnel Management (2008, September). *Structured interviews: A practical guide.* Retrieved from https://apps.opm.gov/ADT/ContentFiles/SIGuide09.08.08.pdf

Wantchekon, L. (2003). Clientelism and voting behavior: Evidence from a field experiment in Benin. *World Politics, 55,* 399–422.

Weyers, M. L., Strydom, H., & Huisamen, A. (2011). Triangulation in social work research: The theory and examples of its practical application. *Social Work, 44,* 207–222.

Wolf, A., Ekman, I., & Dellenborg, L. (2012). Everyday practices at the medical ward: A 16-month ethnographic field study. *BMC Health Services Research, 12*, 1–13.

Zambo, D. (2011). Action research as signature pedagogy in an education doctorate program: The reality and hope. *Innovative Higher Education, 36*, 261–271.

Zangl, B. (2008). Judicialization matters! A comparison of dispute settlement under GATT and the WTO. *International Studies Quarterly, 52*, 825–854.

Index

ⓈSAGE researchmethods

The essential online tool for researchers from the world's leading methods publisher

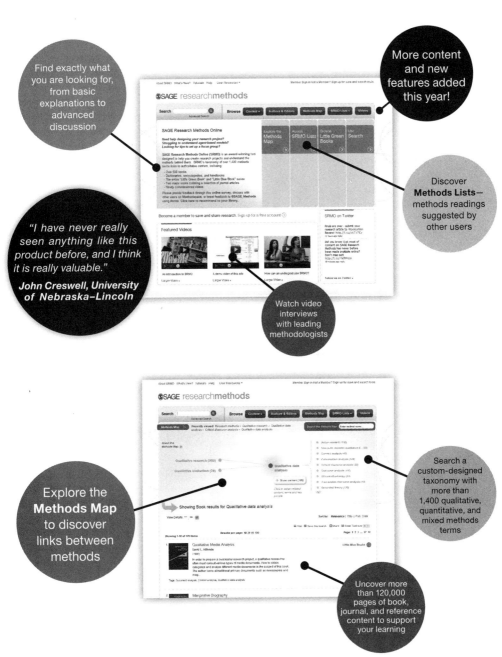

Find exactly what you are looking for, from basic explanations to advanced discussion

More content and new features added this year!

Discover **Methods Lists**— methods readings suggested by other users

"I have never really seen anything like this product before, and I think it is really valuable."

John Creswell, University of Nebraska–Lincoln

Watch video interviews with leading methodologists

Explore the **Methods Map** to discover links between methods

Search a custom-designed taxonomy with more than 1,400 qualitative, quantitative, and mixed methods terms

Uncover more than 120,000 pages of book, journal, and reference content to support your learning

Find out more at www.sageresearchmethods.com